The Willed Curriculum, Unschooling, and Self-Direction

What do love, trust, respect, care, and compassion have to do with learning?

CARLO RICCI

Ricci Publishing

4 Burkston Place, Toronto, Ontario, Canada

Copyright © 2012 Carlo Ricci

All rights reserved.

ISBN: 0987851810
ISBN-13: 978-0987851819

DEDICATION

To Annabel and Karina—with love.

CONTENTS

	Acknowledgments	i
	Foreword	iii
1	Introduction	Pg 1
2	What Others Have Said About Unschooling	Pg 11
3	Strengths of Unschooling	Pg 28
4	Limitations of Unschooling	Pg 43
5	Love and the Willed Curriculum	Pg 57
6	Trust and the Willed Curriculum	Pg 72
7	Respect and the Willed Curriculum	Pg 81
8	Care, Compassion, and the Willed Curriculum	Pg 91
9	The Willed Curriculum	Pg 104
10	The Willed Curriculum: Soulful Spaces	Pg 118
11	Conclusion	Pg 139
	References	Pg 148

ACKNOWLEDGMENTS

First, I wish to thank John Taylor Gatto, Pat Farenga, Kellie Rolstad, Jerry Mintz, Ron Miller, and Mathew Davis for agreeing to be interviewed and for allowing me to share their insights with others. I have benefited from their wisdom and I hope others will feel the same. I also want to thank Pat Farenga, Kellie Rolestad, John Vitale, Conrad Pritscher, and Steven Taylor for taking the time to read a draft version of the book and to provide me with useful feedback and commentary. I would like to thank Pat Farenga once again and this time for his kind and thoughtful foreword. I would also like to thank Stephen Tedesco for his help with his technical skills and the way he manipulates technology as if by magic. I would also like to thank Marian Parish for proofreading the piece. And finally,. although I did not have the pleasure and good fortune of meeting John Holt, I would like to thank him for all he did and for all his works continue to do to move us to a place where we can come to trust learners.

FOREWORD

As a frequent speaker about homeschooling and unschooling, being interviewed at a homeschooling conference is not an uncommon event for me. However, when that interview is recorded, placed on YouTube, then reconsidered and revisited several times by the interviewer, it is an uncommon event. Carlo Ricci has done just that with this book, and as a result he has created a thoughtful meditation and a powerful explication of what Ricci defines broadly as learner-centered democratic education and specifically as unschooling.

During the video interviews Ricci asked each person the same questions, including "How do you define unschooling?" After watching the videos Ricci asked his interview subjects for clarification on some points that they made, adding more depth to these questions. Reading those responses will not provide the reader with a definitive definition or a clear plan of action; as Ricci notes, "In trying to better understand what unschooling means, ultimately the reader will have to do some work and try to fit themselves within the conversation in places where they feel most comfortable. Again, the definition of unschooling is not a closed one, but one that is open and welcoming of diverse positions." Along with the diverse positions about unschooling that you will read in this book, there are commonalities, too, and Ricci does a nice job of showing these.

At a time in our society when children's learning seems to hinge completely on how adults teach them—to the point that we are planning to punish and reward teachers based on their students' test scores—Ricci notes how some concerned parents and educators are actively pursuing the opposite position: Teaching does not produce learning; the activity of learners produces learning. By using this life-based model for helping children learn, many parents, including Ricci, have discovered that not only do their children learn well but that their lives, as individuals, family, and community-members, are enriched as well.

This book will inspire you to respect and honor your child's abilities to learn and to allow your child the time and space to figure out what and how he or she wants to learn. It also delves into topics such as how learner-centered democratic education can help inner-city youth and other populations who are at risk or who are disengaged from their educations; how reading and writing can be learned in longer timeframes and different sequences than conventional school allows; how learner-directed doesn't mean a tyranny of the learner; these, and many other topics, await your discovery.

What do love, trust, respect, care, and compassion have to do with learning? Everything, as you will learn when you read this compassionate and contemplative book.

—Pat Farenga, President Holt Associates. www.holtgws.com
Co-author of Teach Your Own: The John Holt Book of Homeschooling

1 INTRODUCTION

A child, like an adult, learns most and learns best when he or she learns according to his or her will. Following her own will leads to the development of her "willed curriculum," her entirely personal, customized education experience. A small but growing literature focuses on the role of adults in trust-based, holistic, child-controlled, self-organized, self-directed learning, often referred to as unschooling, open inquiry, holistic learning, or life learning, among other terms, which will be defined and discussed in the chapters ahead. Since the learner has ultimate control, she is ready, receptive, willing, and motivated to learn—this is the power of the willed curriculum.

I would like to be clear from the beginning that the learner can invite others to help him or her learn. This relationship is most powerful as long as the learner continues to control the process, and since the learner is in control, she will more likely be appreciative of the help she is getting. This results in a mutually constructive and positive experience for the learner, the "teacher," and the community at large. It is also important that the roles are not set, but fluid. By this I mean that the roles people play within the relationship are not static, but at any point the teacher could be the learner and the learner the teacher. This fluidity contributes to the process being mutually respectful because the parties realize that everyone has knowledge worth sharing and that everyone learns from everyone, even by and from our selves. It's also fluid in the sense that the curriculum and the resources are timely and based on the present context rather than externally imposed, determined, and expected to be followed in a linear process regardless of the needs and wants of the learner, and regardless of what the learner decides is appropriate for the current situation. Clearly, a learner-directed experience is much superior to a preplanned or predetermined recipe, since all learners have different interests and needs and it is they that get to self-organize and self-direct their paths.

I emphasize and recognize that we often count on other people to help us learn. For example, even if we learn by ourselves via computer technology, we often are relying on what other people have posted and constructed. We learn from other people when we read books, watch documentaries, and so on. Not only do we learn from other people, but we also learn from other beings and things as well. The more open and receptive we are, and the more time, freedom, and leisure we have to follow our own interests and wills, the more exciting, deep, and rich learning can be.

As already mentioned, relationally we need to look at the learner/teacher in a more holistic way. Similar to yin and yang, every teacher is a learner and every learner is a teacher. This holistic understanding facilitates a loving, trust-filled, respectful, caring, and compassionate relationship that honors everyone involved.

Throughout this book, my focus is both local and broad. I am thinking about young people and learning while at the same time being fully aware of the importance of community. This book is written with learners of all ages in mind and is for schoolers and unschoolers alike. It is meant for anyone interested in schooling, education, teaching, learning, childrearing, love, trust, respect, care, compassion, and community. It is meant to push, press, squeeze, and nudge mainstream schoolers as well as unschoolers to think about how things can be. It is meant to be provocative and informative and to provide a holistic, learner-centered democratic worldview. Ultimately, it is a book full of hope, love, trust, respect, care, and compassion.

Unschooling is a perfect example of a worldview that is consistent with what I have in mind when I think about the willed curriculum. In short, unschooling is a learner-centered, democratic approach to learning, education, schooling, and living life that is hinged on love, trust, respect, care, and compassion. It is learner centered in that learners decide what they want to learn, when, where, how, and whether they want to participate in the first place. Unschooling is also democratic, since learners have a substantive say in running the spaces and places that they inhabit. As well, the democratic approach involves an inherent balance between individual freedom and community living.

I believe that those of us who subscribe to a holistic learner-centered approach have some powerful narratives that are worth sharing. I believe that both schoolers and unschoolers can learn much from dialoguing and sharing narratives with each other. With respect to schools, some try to change the system from within, and others are showing that there are other ways from without. Schooling has not changed significantly in more than 100 years, and the culture and rituals are so entrenched many believe that the only way to make substantive change is to step outside of the institutional box and to begin anew. It is not enough to tweak or modify how we test or assign, for example, but what we need to do is to understand that these tools can be eliminated altogether with great success, as is common practice among unschoolers and free schoolers, such as the Sudbury Valley Model. We need to move from tweaking practices to questioning the need for various entrenched practices in the first place.

The writing of this book is inspired by hope—the hope that many more will embrace friendlier and gentler practices. My personal experience, research, and exposure to others who are practicing within learner-centered democratic lifestyles has helped me understand the positive potential inherent in this approach. Over the years I have talked with thousands of people who knew either little or nothing about unschooling and learner-centered democratic lifestyles or had an unfortunately negative perception of what these approaches entail, and by the end of our conversation, an overwhelmingly large number of the people I spoke with seemed to better appreciate their potential. This has inspired me to continue to share my experiences and to try to find new ways to reach wider and wider audiences. I am hoping that with this book I can continue to share and help more people to adopt or accept a willed curriculum, or those aspects of the approach which resonate with them. I believe that by better understanding what the willed curriculum is, every person can use the learner-centered democratic worldview to make positive changes for themselves and their communities.

Above all else the willed curriculum is a philosophy, a worldview, and a way of life. We are all guided by a philosophy, whether we are aware of it or not, and by becoming aware of what our philosophy is, we are free to either change our assumptions or to understand the limitations and logical conclusions of our philosophy. I strongly believe that the willed curriculum has had an extremely positive influence on me and my family, and so I feel compelled to share the gift with others.

The willed curriculum, of course, does not mean the same thing to everyone, nor is it a recipe that can be followed formulaically. Throughout this book, I will share with you what the willed curriculum has come to mean to me and how I understand it. Once my understanding of it becomes comprehensible, it is up to others to then decide for themselves whether it will work for them and to rewrite how it can benefit and enhance their lives.

I primarily see myself as a people advocate, and that includes young people. Unfortunately, adults feel authorized to do things to young people that would not be tolerated or accepted if we did the same to any other group. It is shameful that we deny young people freedom of speech and basic dignity and control over their own lives. Those who take the willed curriculum seriously can clearly remedy this injustice. Again, the willed curriculum is about love, trust, respect, care, and compassion, and if these laudable qualities are genuinely embraced and understood in the ways that I understand them, then I believe that all people will be infinitely better off.

I have thought a lot about why some people resist a willed curriculum such as unschooling, and it may have something to do with the word itself. In other words, the term unschooling seems to put many people off, and that is why some prefer terms such as natural learning, life learning, organic learning, self-directed learning, self-organized learning, and so on. Unfortunately, some dismiss worldviews that take the will of the learner seriously, without even taking the time to understand what it means and without ever meeting people who are living and embracing this worldview.

Another reason why some may dismiss unschooling and other willed approaches is because schooling has taken such an ingrained hold within our world. We have come to connect learning and everything good with schooling, despite so much contrary evidence to indicate that schools are failing on so many levels. That schools are not working becomes clear when we see how people who are intimately involved in schools suffer, mentally, emotionally, spiritually, and physically. We see everything from formal and informal dropping out, suicides, bullying, anxiety, depression, complaints of illiteracy and innumeracy, and burnout, to name a few. Schooling may often fail to nourish our bodies, our minds, or our spirits, but it does not have to be this way. So whether you are a schooler or an unschooler, the worldview that I am going to share with you will, if taken seriously, help create a more morally centered and ethical humanity. It is important to remember that for this to benefit you, the world does not have to adopt this worldview; it is enough for you to adopt it. As well, since holism reminds us that everything is integrated, then by simply changing how you act and think, you are making the world a better place for you and for everyone in it. In other words, you are a part of the community, and if you change for the better, then by definition, the world becomes a better place. Many have come to call this positive interconnection "entanglement." In quantum physics, when something is done to an entangled particle, it simultaneously is done to an element of the entangled particle, even though it is many miles away.

To help you better understand where I am coming from and to try to become as transparent as I can be, I want to share with you my philosophical inspirations and share how I have understood and used them for the purposes of writing this book. The worldviews that have had tremendous influences on me are holistic education, critical theory, unschooling, and other approaches that take the will of the learner seriously. Of course, not everyone uses or understands these terms in the same way, so I will share some of what continues to attract me to these philosophies.

Holistic education has taught me to see things as wholes rather than fragmented, discrete units. It has taught me that everything is interconnected and that we need to appreciate our minds, bodies, emotions, and spirits and those of others. It has taught me that we need to respect everything and everyone and understand that everything has a place and a life. It has taught me to value things that we know and things that we cannot know. It has taught me the importance of beginning with our selves in the present. In addition, it has taught me about intuition, contemplation, mindfulness, and soulfulness. It has taught me to value and not be ashamed of love, trust, respect, care, and compassion. It has taught me that I can unfold in beautiful ways and that I need to trust and allow others to do the same. These are things that I have internalized and carry within me. Holistic education and holistic educators have given me and continue to give me the confidence and the power to embrace these values proudly and openly.

Critical theory has opened my eyes to injustices and has given me the support and understanding to do my part to help make the world a better place—to make it less racist, less sexist, less homophobic, less ageist, less classist, less ablest, and so on. It has helped me understand the importance of community and the importance of action. It is not enough to think these things, but we must also act on them if we are truly serious about making changes to ourselves and to the community we inhabit.

At the same time, willed approaches such as unschooling have helped me to understand that all people regardless of age are equally capable of directing their own lives. Unschooling has helped me understand the limitations of our current childrearing practices and the limitations of schooling. Of course all of these philosophies to a certain extent overlap and inform my understanding of learning that is autonomous, self-directed, and that engages. In my mind they are not separate but are whole, interconnected, entangled. They embody and inform each other and overlap.

In what follows I am going to continue to use unschooling as a springboard to share my understanding of the willed curriculum. For so many of us, unschooling makes so much intuitive sense, and it challenges so much of the mistaken certainty of mainstream thinking. Unschooling forces us to rethink assumptions that are deeply ingrained within our bodies, minds, spirits, and emotions. In terms of schooling, it forces us to think about grading, marking, testing, assignments, report cards, externally imposed curriculum, raising hands, bells, classrooms, competition, fear-based teaching, learning, education, child development, and so on. The list is as long as what makes up mainstream schooling. I recognized that for many this is a different way, and because it is so different, many react with caution and resistance, but in my experience, the more people who come to understand unschooling, the more they come to understand about the need to respect a willed curriculum.

In chapter 2 I share the results of a research study I conducted where I asked a number of prominent attendees of the Alternative Education Resource Organization Conference (AERO) about their definitions of unschooling. The interviewees are John Taylor Gatto, Jerry Mintz, Pat Farenga, Ron Miller, Kellie Rolstad, and Mathew Davis. Since unschooling is a type of learner-centered democratic approach, I believe that what they have shared will help us better understand the opportunities resulting from adopting a willed approach to living life. Again, unschooling is one manifestation of a learner-centered democratic approach; others include free schools such as the Sudbury Valley Schools, the Albany Free School, and North Star. The chapter will provide a context to help better understand and hopefully act in ways that are morally and ethically consistent with these approaches. The depth and range of the interviewees' responses continue to help me understand and appreciate unschooling, and so I hope and believe that others will feel the same and ultimately be inspired to act accordingly.

In chapter 3, I again appeal to the same voices that we met in chapter 2 and who were generous enough to share their thoughts and experiences with me. The difference is that this time the focus is on the strength that unschooling offers. The diversity of voices and thoughts powerfully combine and continue to contribute to how unschooling is a philosophical approach from which we can all learn and grow. The strengths that they outline are ones that go beyond unschooling, and are ones that I believe everyone would benefit from adopting.

In chapter 4 I appeal to the same voices to gain some wisdom around the limitations of unschooling. I think that by gaining a better understanding of what these may be, we can be better prepared to avoid them and to think of ways to better embrace the potential that unschooling promises. These limitations and cautions are ones that anyone can and, I believe, will benefit by avoiding.

Chapter 5 is about love and the willed curriculum. In it I argue that we need to act with love and that we need to love our selves and the world at large, and just as important, we need to love what we do. I also argue that we cannot be forced or coerced to love, but love needs to breathe out from within our very core. Furthermore, I share how an externally imposed curriculum is not consistent with what it means to love, how it diminishes the learner's experience and well-being, and therefore how a willed curriculum is well placed to mitigate these pitfalls.

Chapter 6 is about trust and the willed curriculum. Not only is trust in others important, but to learn to trust ourselves is critical. We need to trust that our body, mind, emotions, and spirit will ultimately help guide us to make decisions that are best for both our community in the broadest sense, and for us.

Chapter 7 is about respect and the willed curriculum. The idea is that, as we respect each other, we develop strong bonds and a willingness to listen to try and meet each other's needs. When conflicts arise, it is mostly through respect that they get resolved. And as with love and trust, it is not enough to respect other beings and things, but we must also respect ourselves. By having others respect us, and by respecting others, we come to improve our understanding of the importance of respect in our lives. Like love and trust, respect is also at the core of a willed curriculum.

Chapter 8 is about care and compassion and the willed curriculum. The chapter looks at what a learner-centered democratic worldview that takes care and compassion seriously would look like and how a willed curriculum is entangled with it. By using the word entangled I am trying to convey that although the chapter is about care and compassion, love, trust, and respect are always also present, and the same is true for all of my writing around the willed curriculum. When I write about things separately, ultimately they are not separate, but I write about them that way merely for convenience.

Chapter 9 is about the willed curriculum. In this chapter I say more about the willed curriculum. The willed curriculum allows people to learn about and focus on what they will. The willed curriculum is based in love, trust, respect, care, and compassion, and it focuses on the learner's interest and internal motivation. It is about self-direction, self-organization, and autonomy. It is about the individual and about community. Ultimately, the best context in which to learn things is one where the learner is interested and motivated.

Chapter 10 is titled "The willed curriculum: Soulful places." In this chapter I contrast the spaces within mainstream schooling with those that are learner centered, democratic. I make the appeal for more of us to demand the latter. In this chapter, I use reading as an example of how more young people would enjoy learning something new if they came to it naturally. I share what learning naturally means and looks like.

Throughout the book, I will deal with love, trust, respect, care, and compassion because they play such a big part in understanding what unschooling and the willed curriculum mean to me. I hope in what follows that you will find ways of making use of this gentle, yet powerful worldview and find it as rewarding as my family, so many others, and I have. May the ideas in this book enrich you and your loved ones' lives as much as they have mine.

2 WHAT OTHERS HAVE SAID ABOUT UNSCHOOLING

To better understand what is meant by the willed curriculum, I think it is best to explore what I consider the best example of it in both theory and practice, namely, unschooling. Unschooling is one manifestation of what the willed curriculum captures. The willed curriculum includes other learner-centered democratic approaches and in that sense it is broader than unschooling. One thing that they all have in common is that they capture the will of the learner. In the broadest sense, the willed curriculum can take as many forms as there are learners. In an effort to better understand unschooling, this chapter will bring in some other voices that are familiar with unschooling to help us gain a more varied perspective.

Between June 24 and 27, 2010 I attended the Alternative Education Resource Organization's 7th annual conference in Albany, New York. Before leaving I requested and received permission and approval from both the conference organizers and Nipissing University's ethics review board to conduct research. I decided that while I was there I would ask some prominent thinkers for their thoughts on four questions. I did this with the assistance of two coinvestigators (Rocco Ricci and Stephen Tedesco). The questions I asked were the following:

1. How would you define or explain unschooling to someone?

2. What are the strengths of unschooling?
3. What are the weaknesses of unschooling?
4. Different people use different terms to refer to a similar concept. For example, John Taylor Gatto refers to open source learning, Ron Miller to holistic education or organic learning, Wendy Priesnitz refers to life learning. There is also natural learning, unschooling, and so on. Do you have a preferred term?

For their complete responses to these questions visit the Unschooling Channel at the following address: http://www.youtube.com/UnschoolingChannel

In what follows I will share just brief snippets of the well-articulated, powerful, and important responses given by the interviewees. Their responses have really helped me and others better understand the concept of unschooling. First, I will begin with John Taylor Gatto's response to the first question about how he would define or explain unschooling to someone.

Gatto is a former schoolteacher with nearly 30 years of experience. He has written a number of influential books including *Dumbing us Down: The Hidden Curriculum of Compulsory Schooling* (New Society Publishers, 2005), *Weapons of Mass Instruction: A Schoolteachers' Journey Through the Dark World of Compulsory Schooling* (New Society Publishers, 2009), and *The Underground History of American Education: An Intimate Investigation into the Prison of Modern Schooling* (Oxford Village Press, 2003). Gatto is also a successful and sought-after public speaker. In 1991, while still a New York State teacher, Gatto famously quit teaching in an Op Ed piece he wrote for the *Wall Street Journal* claiming that he was no longer willing to hurt children by teaching them. I have had the pleasure of hearing Gatto speak on a number of occasions, and I had the pleasure of spending some time with him when he was gracious enough to fly to Toronto and then meet me in Brantford, Ontario, where he came to speak to my class of graduate students. The graduate classes are typically capped at 20 and meet in a small room; I had shared the news with some people that he was coming, and by the time John arrived, we had to move venues several times and ultimately had over 200 people come to listen to Gatto's words.

I will deal only with the first question in this chapter namely, how the interviewees would explain or define unschooling to someone, and will address questions 2 and 3 dealing with the strengths and limitations of unschooling, in the next two chapters. So, with respect to the question of "How would you define unschooling?" Gatto (2010a, September 9) replied:

> Unschooling generically is whatever is opposed to building the time you spend developing your mind and character in an unschooled fashion. It is not one thing, it varies . . . . Unschooling means anything that reduces schooling to a minimum use of time. Now, schooling has some value, it just does not have supreme value . . . . You can be schooled to do a lot of things, but you can't be educated to take control of your life; only through unschooling can you do that. (John Taylor Gatto on Unschooling—Part 1)

From Gatto's response we can begin to understand what unschooling is. We begin to see that unschooling is not one thing and that it varies; hence there is a lot of flexibility, overlap, and variation. Gatto goes on to make the point that unschooling reduces schooling to a minimum use of time. So, just because you go to school does not mean you cannot unschool, and similarly, just because you do not go to school does not mean that you are an unschooler. Unschooling is much more complicated and nuanced. We can also glean from what Gatto tells us that schooling and education are not the same things and that if you want to take control of your life unschooling is the way. In sum, then, so far we have a definition of unschooling that suggests that it is not one thing, it varies, it keeps schooling to a minimum, and it helps you take control of your own life.

Another person I interviewed was Ron Miller. Ron Miller is recognized internationally as one of the major thinkers and activists within the field of holistic education. He has written or edited nine books and authored numerous articles, chapters, and book reviews. His books include *What are Schools for? Holistic*

Education in American Culture (Holistic Education Press, 1990), *Free Schools, Free People: Education and Democracy After the 1960s* (State University of New York Press, 2002), and most recently, *The Self-Organizing Revolution: Common Principles of the Educational Alternatives Movement* (Psychology Press/Holistic Education Press, 2008).

In response to the question about how he would define or explain unschooling to someone, Ron Miller (2010, September 9) said,

Unschooling is the decision to pursue learning and growth outside of the structure of schooling. It's a critique of our culture in saying that learning is really a natural human endeavor and does not need to be managed, and shaped, and controlled the way our culture does to most all aspects of life. It's a way of stepping out, or as I like to say, seceding from the institutions of our culture.

Miller clearly points out that learning is a natural human endeavor. From this I would add that learning could take place anytime, anywhere. I would agree with Ron that unschooling is based on the premise that learning does not have to be externally managed. In fact, learners are in the best position to manage their own learning.

Where there may be some disagreement with Miller's statement is around the issue of schooling. In other words, does the broader definition of unschooling presume that those who define themselves as unschoolers cannot attend a formal school setting? Some may argue this, but many people that I know who define themselves as unschoolers do attend formal school settings for some things and at some time. Here is where Gatto's point (that unschooling varies and is not one thing) will help in allowing for unschoolers to attend school and still be considered unschoolers. Strictly speaking, I think that Miller is correct in saying that unschooling is the decision to pursue learning outside of school; however, I see unschooling to be much broader, and I embrace the philosophical spirit of choice behind unschooling as being central to an understanding of unschooling. So in my mind, if someone attends a school, then she is not automatically disqualified from being an unschooler. This is not to say that Miller is wrong and that I am correct, but it just highlights the complexity and variability in how people live unschooling. This will come up again later, and I think that Kellie Rolstad makes a good point; we will see her response in more detail later. She suggests if the learner decides to attend school, then it seems reasonable that simply attending does not negate her or him from being unschoolers. I bring this up because I think that these nuances helps us clarify and bring us closer to thinking about what unschooling can mean to us. As well, I think the issue of attending school is an important one, and it is an issue that comes up again and again in many online groups of which I am a member. Ultimately, it becomes even more complicated, if by going to school, the learner is then expected to give up control of her learning. I believe that the best learning environments will ensure that the learner remains in control, but in our mainstream system this, unfortunately, is rarely the case. This makes Miller's point even stronger, I think, and continues to complicate the issues.

Since I struggle with the question of whether an unschooler can attend school and still be able to self-identify as one, I decided to email Miller and ask him about it. In the email I wrote to him the following:

> During the YouTube interview you started by saying that "unschooling is the decision to pursue learning and growth outside of the structure of schooling." Can you please clarify this, i.e. does this mean that if you attend formal schooling you are then not defined as an unschooler, or unschoolers cannot engage in any formal schooling, or do you see unschooling as a broader philosophical approach and so if someone decides to attend formal schooling and defines themselves as an unschooler, and is learner-centered democratic—then they are still unschooling? i.e., if the learner chooses to do this then . . . .

Miller's thoughtful response is worth sharing. He provided the following response:

I don't think our terminology should be too restrictive, but it does need to have some firm meaning. If an "unschooler" who is for the most part learning in real world situations wants to pursue some learning in a conventional place, they can still call themselves an unschooler or whatever they want. Generally speaking, though, to me the term does imply that a person is pursuing a significant amount of one's learning outside of institutional settings. It doesn't make much sense to practice unschooling inside a school; I don't know what the term would mean in that case. (Personal communication, Friday, October 1, 2010)

In trying to better understand what unschooling means, ultimately the reader will have to do some work and try to fit him/herself within the conversation in places where they feel most comfortable. Again, the definition of unschooling is not a closed one but one that is open and welcoming of diverse positions. So, the hope at the end of this chapter is not that we come to a conclusive definition but that we come to better understand what unschooling means, which is very different, and perhaps in many respects much more important. So, for me, unschooling is a much richer, more complicated philosophy of learning and of life than what can be had in a mainstream school. If an unschooler chooses to attend a mainstream school, then that decision needs to be respected. Having said that, I think that Miller's point is an important one to keep in mind when thinking about unschooling, especially given that so much of mainstream schooling is undemocratic and not learner centered. So, can someone choose to be in a situation that contravenes much of the essence of unschooling and still be an unschooler? This is the question with which I, and perhaps others, have to continue struggling.

Some may suggest that an unschooler who schools fits nicely with the willed curriculum. Think of a situation where a person could be schooled, and their attitude is that the teacher is not in charge of their learning. In this case, the fact that their will determines their curriculum may cause conflict. In other words, the school can claim it's providing the curriculum, but it isn't—not for this child. Or think of a case where the child mentally sidesteps, ignores, the school-provided curriculum, then this child maybe can remain in school unmolested as long as this rebellion is not overt. In essence, the less the child kowtows to the school's curriculum, the more one could claim this schooled child is actually unschooled, since unschooling is an attitude, a philosophy, not a fact about where the child spends her time. I recognize that the term unschooling may get in the way in these cases, and maybe there is a better term, perhaps the willed curriculum. Ultimately, I think we have to continue to have conversations with learners who choose to attend mainstream schools about unschooling as a philosophy in comparison to the mainstream schooling philosophy, so that they can remain critical about their experiences.

Rolstad shared with me that her class Skyped with Wendy Priesnitz, who remarked that free schools are not at all free because attendance is required and that she doesn't think a free school permits life learning. Others may disagree, of course, but it shows how there is a definite continuum from radical unschooling on one end to free schools, to public schools that permit democratic participation of kids, to conventional schools, to . . . military schools; I suppose, pushing it further, to slaves growing up in a slave society. If unschooling is held to be a philosophy, a state of mind that can be maintained no matter what, then presumably an unschooler could attend military school or grow up as a slave and become a highly literate free thinker, like Frederick Douglass perhaps. Ultimately I think that we cannot dictate to the learner what counts as worthwhile for them, and if unschooling is not about the learner, then what is it about? I am afraid that it will move from what the learner wants to what unschooling as a curriculum or philosophy demands. Although this is very tricky, I think we cannot let theory get in the way of the learner's will.

Ultimately, many of us want similar things for our children: We want them to be happy; healthy; respectful of themselves, others, the environment, and everything within the world; we want them to be self-sufficient, confident, and so on. The question is, what is the best way to get there? My response is the willed curriculum, more broadly, and unschooling as an example of this way of life. Again, for me, love, compassion, care, trust, and respect are such a central part of the willed curriculum that if we are unschooling with these ideas at the fore, the rest follows, and if it does not, then we need to continue to dialogue. In fact, I see it as a process, not an end, and so we need to continue to provoke and challenge each other to do better ethically and morally. It makes little sense to impose and grade how environmental someone is being; we need to allow them to live it through for it to be meaningful.

Of course, there are those who would disagree and argue that if we want young people to be respectful of the environment, we need to create formal school lessons that are graded and assignments to ensure that students understand the concepts. Some would champion backwards planning, where we know where we want young people to be, and then we create a plan and assign, assess, and ensure that they comply with how we want them to be. I believe that there is a better and gentler approach; I believe that unschooling will get us there in a more powerful way. I believe that through unschooling, young people will not only comply when other people are around, but they will develop an embodied and internal understanding of what it means to be happy; healthy; respectful of themselves, others, the environment, and everything within the world; they will more likely become self-directing, confident, and so on. In short, I believe that many of the things we want young people to embody are best achieved through freedom rather than coercion, restriction, and violence.

I believe that it is not through coercion but through love, respect, compassion, and trust that young people will be the type of people we would like to see more of within our world. It is no coincidence that many people have the perception that unschoolers are hippie types: vegan, environmentally conscious, peaceful, and loving. Of course not all unschoolers fit this stereotype, but I believe there is a correlation between unschooling and what I will call hipness, not hippieness. It could be that hip people are attracted to unschooling as a philosophy, or that unschooling as a philosophy inspires hipness; the truth is likely somewhat of a more complicated holistic interconnection in that one can be separate from the other only in theory but that they are intertwined in practice. Hipness is an interesting concept and is often used in music. A formalized classical musician who plays from the music and is not very creative is considered very "square" by jazz musicians. Within the realm of jazz (where improvisation is paramount), a great solo is often called "hip," and in my case I am suggesting that it is full of love, compassion, respect, and so on. This is very similar to the way I see unschooling. We need to allow people to live their lives as they see fit and not be a note within someone else's music.

In sum, Miller adds to our understanding of unschooling by pointing out that unschooling is a critique of our culture; learning is really a natural human endeavor and does not need to be managed, shaped, and controlled. And finally, he adds that unschooling is a way of stepping out or seceding from the institutions of our culture. Given everything else that Miller posits, I would add that seceding does not mean breaking away from our world but embracing it and understanding it in a more natural way. Let's now move on to Pat Farenga and see how his thoughts on the definition of unschooling will continue to help us understand what unschooling can mean.

Patrick Farenga worked closely with the author and teacher John Holt for 4 years, until Holt's death in 1985. Farenga is currently the President of Holt Associates Inc. and was the Publisher of *Growing Without Schooling* magazine (GWS) from 1985 until it ceased publication in November 2001. His most recent book is *Teach Your Own: The John Holt Book of Homeschooling* (DaCapo Press, May 2003), a revised, updated version of Holt's original text.

When I asked Farenga (2010, September 9) how he would define or explain what unschooling is to someone, he responded:

My simple definition is that unschooling is allowing your children as much freedom to learn from and about the world as you can comfortably bear as their parent, and that varies from family to family. Some are going to be very liberal and others are going to be only liberal in certain areas, and that's the beauty of unschooling to me.

Farenga highlights an important tension. It seems that according to Farenga, unschooling still places the supreme authority on the parents. This may simply be a given within the world in which we live. In other words, ultimately even if young people are given a say about substantive decisions they need to make, it is up to the parents or the state to grant this. Nevertheless, I would like to think that unschooling is about finding ways to democratize the power relationship within families in such a way that young people are truly self-directed and not simply given an artificial voice.

I thought that, given the importance and centrality of parenting within the unschooling process, I would email Farenga the following request for clarification:

> I am hoping you can clarify something for me. In the YouTube video you say, "My simple definition is that unschooling is allowing your children as much freedom to learn from and about the world as you can comfortably bear as their parent, and that varies from family to family." What role does the children's freedom play in this and in unschooling? Does this mean that the parents have authority over the children? i.e., Isn't unschooling trying to create a more democratic and level playing field, rather than parental hierarchy—if you know what I mean?

Farenga responded with the following:

> My definition is meant to defuse the common assumption that unschooling makes the child the primary focus of the family, all-powerful in their demands, and that parents merely act as their wish-givers. I'm including the concept of give and take, family dynamics, and social interaction in my definition. Perhaps I should work at fine-tuning my definition. But that's

my thinking behind it. (Personal communication, 26 October 2010)

I think we are in agreement on this point, and what he says is crucial for me in my understanding of unschooling. Unschooling is about a give and take (like yin yang). It is not simply parents sacrificing themselves to their children's wishes. It is democratic in the sense that everyone's needs have to be considered, and given sufficient consideration. So from Farenga's definition we can take that unschooling is about allowing people as much freedom to learn from, and about, the world in a way that is about give and take.

Hopefully the variety and quality of responses offered by the various people so far is starting to present a clearer picture of what unschooling could mean and how it can be practiced. Above all, I think that this shows that there are some critical areas that need to be clarified and that we need to continue to think about and build on. Although there will always be disagreements, I think airing critical differences is a healthy way to move unschooling forward. I will share a few more responses, with the hope that unschooling will begin to become even clearer still, and thereby also shedd insight into the willed curriculum. Next we turn to Jerry Mintz.

For over 30 years Jerry Mintz has been a leading voice in the alternative school movement. He was a public school teacher for 17 years. He was also a public and independent alternative school principal and has founded several alternative schools and organizations. In addition, he has lectured and consulted around the world.

He was the first executive director of the National Coalition of Alternative Community Schools (NCACS) and was a founding member of the International Democratic Education Conference (IDEC). In 1989, he founded the Alternative Education Resource Organization. He continues to serve as AERO's director and as the Managing Editor of AERO's networking magazine, *The Education Revolution*.

Mintz has made several appearances on national radio and TV

shows. His essays, commentaries, and reviews have appeared in numerous newspapers, journals, and magazines including *The New York Times*, *Newsday*, *Paths of Learning*, *Green Money Journal*, *Communities*, *Saturday Review*, *Holistic Education Review*, as well as the anthology *Creating Learning Communities* (Foundation for Educational Renewal, 2000).

His publications include the *Handbook of Alternative Education* (Macmillan, 1994) and the *Almanac of Education Choices* (Macmillan/Simon & Schuster, 1995) where he was Editor-in-Chief. He is the author of *No Homework and Recess All Day: How to Have Freedom and Democracy in Education* (Bravura, 2003) and coedited *Turning Points: 35 Visionaries in Education Tell Their Own Stories* (AERO, 2010) with Carlo Ricci.

Mintz (2010, September 9) defines unschooling in the following way:

Well, I think that the concept of unschooling is based on the idea that kids are natural learners. And I think that that is a very basic paradigm as opposed to the idea that kids are naturally lazy and need to be forced to learn. So, if you assume that kids are natural learners, then the purpose of unschooling is really to follow the interest of the learner and be there as a resource for them.

I think that Mintz underscores some very important ideas. First, that people are natural learners. The question then becomes, if people are natural learners, then what role is there for others to play? His response is that given that they are natural learners, they need to follow their interests and others need to be there as resources for them. I take this to mean that others need to be there to respond to the needs of the learner when the learner asks for assistance and to provide only the assistance that is requested and wanted. In other words, being a resource means that you are very aware of the relationship you are in with the other and that you do not impose, manipulate, or force the other to learn what you may believe is best for the other. Of course, you can suggest, but ultimately the learner needs to be a willing participant and the curriculum needs to be a willed curriculum.

As mentioned earlier, Kellie Rolstad will add to the discussion about whether a person who chooses to go to school can be considered an unschooler, and it is to her that we turn next. Kellie Rolstad is an associate professor at Arizona State University who conducts research in unschooling, homeschooling, and democratic education. Professor Rolstad holds a PhD in Education from UCLA, has served as a visiting scholar at Harvard University's Graduate School of Education, and has organized numerous academic symposia on unschooling and democratic education at such venues as the American Association for the Advancement of Curriculum Studies, the American Educational Research Association, the Annual Local to Global Justice Teach In, and the Narrative, Arts-Based and "Post" Approaches to Research (NAPAR). She has published numerous articles and book chapters, appearing in prestigious journals such as *Educational Policy*, *Teachers College Record*, *Bilingual Research Journal*, *Bilingual Review*, and *Hispanic Journal of Behavioral Sciences*. She has served on the Board of Directors of Phoenix Rising, a democratic free school project located in Phoenix, Arizona, and is currently unschooling her three children. Rolstad (2010, September 9) defines unschooling in the following way:

> I tell people that it's living and learning without a script. Just the way any adult would live their life, what they do on a daily basis or what they do with any kind of long-term plan is completely their own. So, I think that respecting and trusting children to do the same thing is unschooling. Now, I always say that I unschool as an adult, that I am unschooling my children, but I always say that my children self-school . . . They make the decisions. My 13-year-old takes college classes. Some people would say that if a child decides to go to school they are not unschooled, but if it's their choice, it's kind of a grey area.

With reference to her first point about how unschooling is living and learning without a script, I would clarify that there could be a script, but the script is not an externally imposed one and that it can be modified or changed as one goes along. In other words, it is a willed curriculum. And I think that Rolstad makes an important point when she says that the script is completely their own. Her points about respecting and trusting children are very central to my understanding of unschooling as well, and she is right on when she points out that whether a child who attends school can be an unschooler is a grey area, as we discussed earlier.

Rolstad goes on to offer a nice example to help us better understand and appreciate the role of curriculum within an unschooling worldview. She states,

> My daughter, who is 11, said that she really wished she had a tree in our backyard that she could climb, and I said why don't you climb that fort that we have that was installed for climbing? And she said, but it's made for climbing. It has handles all over it. The fun of climbing trees is that you never know when you are going to fall. And then she said, some branches snap, some branches wobble, and some are unexpectedly strong. And I wrote that down word for word because I thought wow, that whole speech just came out of her and she had really given it a lot of thought about what is so fun about climbing trees, and I think that's exactly what a curriculum is to a kid too. It's giving him the handles, it's telling him how to climb a tree, and that's not the fun of it. The fun of it is doing it for yourself, exploring it yourself, finding out for yourself which branches snap or wobble or are unexpectedly strong. And if I tell her, these are the sources that you should use for your learning, then I am showing her the strong branches. I want her to find out for herself which sources are weak and which sources will wobble and which sources are unexpectedly strong . . . . So I think for me the strength of unschooling . . . each person doing their own thing, authoring their own life, but without a script.

I think that this is a nice example for what curriculum within an unschooling context could be. From my perspective, I would clarify that it is not about isolating people, nor is it about not helping them even if they ask for help for fear that they would then not find out for themselves. And when I shared this with Rolstad, she said, "Right. I would never say it's about isolating people or not helping them even if they ask for help either." Rather, I would suggest that it is more organic and natural, and so we do not need to create artificial, disconnected curricula that do not interest the learner and then develop ways to control and manipulate the learner to comply; instead, we can trust and respect and help when asked in any way that we can. In other words, we can appeal to others to help us learn, but we need to direct and keep control of what that looks like.

Mathew Davis grew up in Indianapolis and began community organizing when he was 14, and he began public speaking at age 15. Although he attended public schools his entire life, he has been critical of the ones he attended throughout his schooling career. He has expressed that his vocation is focused on social justice and simply helping people survive.

I first met and heard Mathew Davis speak at the AERO conference. It was clear to me that what he had to share was very special. He was talking from embodied experience. I took from his speech that he was an unsuccessful and disinterested student whose life is an example of how someone can attend school and yet still unschool himself. He would likely not say this about himself, but I fit what he said within my framework. He is very bright, articulate, but his schoolteachers did not see him that way. He was strong enough to see through the myths that they were trying to teach him, and he forged his own learning. He searched and continues to search for his own truths, like many of us do, in spite of the obstacle that school proved to be for him.

As Davis was speaking, I was reminded of my own history and struggles with mainstream schooling. I was reminded about how I did not get into postsecondary education when I first applied to university because my grades were too low, and then how ultimately I did get in after attending a semester of college (in Canada colleges are technical, practical schools—although this is changing in that some colleges are now offering degrees) and then using those marks to reapply to university and eventually getting in. Of course, unfortunately I did not know then what I know now about open universities and other alternative paths to entering university for those who choose to (see Ricci, 2008). Despite my lack of awareness, I did stumble on one of many alternative paths, and in the end I ended up being a "successful" university student.

Ultimately, it took me one year to complete my master's degree, and for all intents and purposes one year to complete my PhD while I was working as a full-time English high school teacher. I share this not to brag, but just to show how wrong schools can be about what potential the people within their walls possess when they choose to accomplish something. I have to add that even as a masters and PhD student, I still felt that school was an obstacle. I could not learn what I wanted to learn, and I had to read their books and answer their questions, which I did robotically while grasping and reading what I really wanted to read in the little spare time I had left. It was only when I was not in schooling that my education and learning truly flourished. Davis's story reminded me of this and so much more. When I asked Davis (2010, September 10) about how he would define unschooling, he said,

> Unschooling is kids taking their own initiative with their education in general as far as life is concerned. Taking it in their own hands, being proactive with it. I think that's the beauty of unschooling. Natural learning, holistic education is that it's all about you and it's your own initiative, your own drive, your own passion. You're self-determined.

Although Davis is correct in that unschooling does respect the individual, the point I add is that individuals always live within social contexts and so the community is always a part of the individual. In a holistic sense the two cannot be separated and cannot be ignored. I have met many, many unschoolers and have been to numerous unschooling, free schooling, and learner-centered democratic events, and it is clear to me that overwhelmingly these people care deeply about their world and their communities. Given this, it is very difficult to argue that unschooling leads to the individual ignoring community, when in practice, this is not the case.

Davis adds to our understanding by pointing out that unschooling is about a person's own initiative, drive, passion, and that the person is self-determined.

After thinking, reflecting, and contemplating on the above responses and my own prior experiences, this is a brief description of how I have come to understand unschooling and thereby the willed curriculum. Unschooling is a learner-centered democratic approach to learning and living life. It is about care, compassion, love, trust and respect. It is not one thing; it varies and it helps you take control of your own life. Unschooling is a critique of our culture, and learning is really a natural human endeavor and does not need to be managed, and shaped, and controlled. Unschooling is about allowing people as much freedom to learn from and about the world in a way that is about give and take. It recognizes that we are natural learners who need to follow our interests, and others need to be there as resources for us. It's about following our own script. It is about a person's own initiative, drive, passion, and it understands and insists that we ought to be self-determined.

In the next two chapters, our understanding of the willed curriculum will continue to deepen as we explore it further when looking at what Gatto, Mintz, Farenga, Miller, Rolstad, and Davis consider to be the strengths and limitations of unschooling.

3 STRENGTHS OF UNSCHOOLING

A good way to come to better understand something is to come to understand its perceived strengths and weaknesses, so in the next two chapters it is sensible to consider the strengths and limits of unschooling. Considering strengths is important because it offers hope and inspiration. It advances our understanding and appreciation for what an unschooling worldview can offer. It offers a justification and allows us to better appreciate why unschooling is so important. Limitations are equally important because they offer cautions and a guide to tread carefully and find ways and choose paths that can improve on what others warn against.

To help better understand unschooling's strengths we will begin with Gatto. In outlining strengths Gatto (2010b, September 9) states the following:

> If you have your wits about you, you can in fact investigate yourself, your neighborhood, the history that appeals to you, and you can figure out what parts of it you want to reproduce in your unschooling experience. You can, in fact, teach the way children learn. And not to say everybody who unschools takes advantage of that, but I would say, I have been doing this speaking around the world for 20 years, and I would say the majority of the people who unschool, not the majority of the people who home school, but those who unschool, in fact, hit

on a custom-tailored formula that worked for boy A and girl B. Actually, girl A and boy B are the chief architects of what occurs in unschooling.

Teaching to the way children learn is a tremendous strength of unschooling. In my own unschooling experience this has been the case. My children both learned how to read and write in their own way. They both used what worked for them at the time. I believe what they did was so effective because they were doing what they willed. They were following their interests and passions and were figuring things out as they went along. They did not both have to follow a similar pattern, and, in fact, because they did not, I believe it made the experience so much more valuable for them. If I had to get them to follow someone else's idea of how to learn to read and write, for example, that would not have met their needs in the same way.

Similarly, if I imposed on them and forced them to do activity X at 9 a.m. and activity B at 9:45 there would inevitably be conflict and resistance. Instead they learned how to read and write at their own pace in their own ways. Some of the ways I am aware of, and some I am not, and I suspect that there are others of which even they may not be aware. They learned mostly simply by living life and by reading and writing because it was meaningful for them at the time, and not because they wanted to learn to read and write just for the sake of learning to read and write. They learned to read and write because what they willed to do demanded that they read and write. They learned to do things as the need arose. For example, they wanted to write birthday cards, notes, lists, and journals; and they wanted to read signs, words on the screen, words in books, and words that appeared in the world around them. Each step of the way, they took the lead, and they were the architects of their own willed curriculum.

Hopefully, you will agree that this is a much more powerful way of learning to read and write, or doing anything else for that matter, than imposing a standardized formula that may or may not work on a particular individual. Perhaps schoolers believe that they do not have a choice given economic and logistic constraints, but if they want to do what is best for children, they need to rethink how they do things. I refer to reading and writing as an example because so many are so obsessed with reading and writing. But in truth my children have learned so much more. They have learned everything from cooking and chores to playing the piano, and from skating and art to singing and swimming. Not only is it invaluable that people learn in their own way, but also that they get the respect to work at their own pace. Some can learn to read and write at an earlier age, while others at a later age. They learned these things on their own and with the assistance of others, but they always remain the architects of their journey. Unschooling respects that difference and does not see learning to read later as a deficit. In support of allowing children to learn at their own pace, in her book *Free Range Learning: How Homeschooling Changes Everything*, Weldon (2010) writes,

> A study conducted in the 1930s followed children who received formal reading instruction at different ages. Initially the early readers had an advantage when tested, although that disappeared by fourth grade. By their teens a more significant difference emerged. The children who were taught to read later were more spontaneous and enthusiastic readers than those taught earlier. Recent research echoes these results. (p. 231)

She goes on to cite some of the more recent studies, and here is what she says about one of them:

> The study's authors, Karen Keys and William Crain found that many children received little or no systematic teaching yet read at or above age level by eight years old. Those who were not reading at age level by eight years old tended to catch up by age eleven. (p. 231)

She then quotes the authors of the study, who conclude that the goal of the parents to instill a love of reading was successful in that they enjoyed reading very much. To me this is much more important than high test scores. At my local neighborhood school, for example, the children scored above provincial and board average in reading but reported below board and provincial average in their enjoyment of reading. So what is the point of receiving high test scores if ultimately the children do not enjoy reading? This is the danger of schooling that is mitigated by unschooling. By having the freedom to read what and when they like, and when it is meaningful to them, children see reading as a positive thing, not an externally imposed chore. You do not need to be tested and forced to prove your competence in order to learn to read. Learning to read can and does happen in much more gentle, meaningful, and relevant ways.

If you recall, in sharing his thoughts on the advantages of unschooling, Gatto (2010a, September 9) also pointed out that "if you have your wits about you, you can in fact investigate yourself, your neighborhood, the history that appeals to you, and you can figure out what parts of it you want to reproduce in your unschooling experience." This too is a tremendous advantage. Imagine being able to spend time investigating yourself, your neighborhood, and the history that appeals to you, and then being able to create your schooling experience based on this. Being able to understand yourself, your neighborhood, and your history and engaging with what resonates most with you is clearly a superior experience to following someone else's agenda. In addition, Gatto's point highlights the connection between the self and community that is so important to my idea of unschooling. Unschooling is not about isolating us from the world, but it is about finding our place within it. This is a point eloquently made by Miller, to whom we turn next.

In speaking of unschooling strengths, R. Miller (2010) says,

If you trust human nature and you think that we do naturally learn, that we have the resources with ourselves to reach out to the world and engage with the world and grow through that experience, then unschooling gives people the opportunity to do that. It allows the most natural organic processes of our development to thrive, to have space to grow. In the institutions that have been fashioned around learning, that often gets throttled, so unschooling is a way of releasing our natural potentials. I think also it accommodates the vast differences between human beings. People learn in different ways at different paces and for different reasons, and when you are in an institution that is trying to standardize things and make everything efficient, you lose that diversity, and so unschooling allows individuals to be themselves and to pursue the rhythm that is most natural to them; unschooling is a way of releasing our natural potentials.

Miller's word choice clearly underscores unschooling's strengths. For example, the following points he makes increase the attraction of it for me, specifically, when he says that it allows the most natural organic processes of our development to thrive; to have space to grow; people learn in different ways at different paces and for different reasons; to pursue the rhythm that is most natural to them; and that unschooling is a way of releasing our natural potentials. These points inspire me to continue to advocate for unschooling and other learner-centered democratic approaches. The description of unschooling gains even more strength especially when contrasted with what Miller says about schooling: "When you are in an institution that is trying to standardize things and make everything efficient, you lose that diversity. In the institutions that have been fashioned around learning, that often gets throttled." Again, if schools want to become relevant, they need to heed the strengths of unschooling and find ways to implement them within the everyday realities experienced by those within its domain. When I say those, I mean the students, but also the adults and anyone else who is directly and indirectly connected with schooling, which at some point is all of us; ultimately, we all have a stake in what schools do or do not do. Next we look at how Farenga describes the strengths of unschooling.

Pat Farenga (2010, September 9) says,

The strengths of unschooling are obviously you are working with a child's ability, that they want to learn something, so you are working with a willing learner. So that is one of the strengths. Another strength is that you as a parent are [not] acting as the teacher who has to know everything, who has to have everything planned in advance and has to know what's going to happen, and instead you are a facilitator, you're learning alongside, then using your experience and your knowledge of the world to provide them sort of a map where to go. But they are going to follow the map, they are going to do the walking, the discovery, and that to me is a very big strength. You don't necessarily know where it's going to go, but you're there with them to help, you're not just there like Svengali saying go forth and learn math, use this textbook, follow this procedure. And finally, I can go on and on about strength, but I am trying to limit it to three, and the third one is that it promotes family unity. Even in a single-child family, because unschooling necessitates dialogue between the parent and the child and the larger community. In order to find out if a child has an interest in working with animals, and you know nothing about animals, the two of you go out into the community and find what resources there are and go from there, and that's a bonding experience. You're not a teacher from whom all knowledge pours forth, and you're [not] sort of an ATM of knowledge dispensing to kids as they punch the numbers in; instead, you're modeling learning behavior for them, and I think that is very powerful. If your children see how you respond in situations that you don't know how to respond, you're giving them a very important lesson: This is how we learn something that we don't know anything about.

Farenga makes some very worthwhile arguments that we should welcome when considering the strengths of unschooling. Some should sound familiar to us by now and others are mentioned for the first time. Unschooling allows us to deal with willing learners and to work within their ability. Although the parents are the facilitators, the learners do the walking and the discovery. So, this is not to say that if a learner has a question we ignore that question and insist that the learners go off and discover the answers on their own. What it does mean is that we build and develop natural relationships. So if I know something and someone asks me a question about it, I can then genuinely and honestly help the learner in any way that I can. For example, recently my younger daughter, who is now 5, has decided that she wants to write and draw in her journal more consistently. When she does this she wants me to be with her so that if there is a word that she wants to spell and is not sure of how to spell it, she can ask me. This goes against much of what I was taught as a teacher candidate in a faculty of education. I was told that I should let them just guess how to spell words or ask them to consult a dictionary. Perhaps, given that the schooling relationship is not a one-to-one ratio, this may be how it needs to be; however, I can think of ways even within schools to ensure that this becomes a one-to-one ratio. For example, if schools had an environment that was open and multiage, it would allow more people to be available if someone wanted to find a resource. This would allow those who could spell better to help those who can spell less well. Of course, this happens often in peer-directed/cooperative learning within formal schooling; specifically, that many teachers pair up strong and weak students together for this very reason. Unfortunately, in many cases mainstream schools are very formal and traditional where, in some cases, students are sitting in rows and are not allowed to speak freely. And even where mainstream classrooms are more progressive, this criticism is still valid because ultimately the power still rests with others and not with the learners, and so since others decide when and where and who and so on, self-organizing how one learns to read and write, for example, is virtually impossible. In addition, tests, level books, an external curriculum, myths about developmental stages that suggest everyone needs to learn X by the time they reach Y, myths about children and what they are capable of, and myths about children and their desire to learn all compound the difficulty to practice self-directed, autonomous, and engaged learning.

It was clear that my daughter did not want to misspell words and she wanted me to tell her how to spell them correctly. She recognized that this is important, and she wanted me to support her with this goal of hers. When she asked how do you spell X, I simply answered the question. I did not play a schooling game of teacher and student where I asked her to sound it out first, nor did I give her a lesson in phonetics, I simply answered her question. Naturally, by doing this, her spelling has improved and so has her reading, because reading and writing are intimately connected. She goes back and rereads what she has written and she looks back to find words that she has forgotten how to spell, and that she has previously written, to see how they are spelled. Again the relationship needs to be natural and genuine. I believe that having a teacher ask a student to phonetically sound out a word is not natural and genuine in the same ways. It is a different approach and, in my mind, an artificial approach. For my daughter, the important part in all of this is that she was in control and her activities were authentic. Holt (1999) makes this clear in the following example.

> Almost a century later John Dewey was to talk about "learning by doing." The way for students to learn (for example) how pottery is made is not to read about it in a book but to make pots. Well, OK, no doubt about its being better. But making pots just to learn how it is done still doesn't seem to me anywhere near as good as making pots (and learning from it) because *someone needs pots*. The incentive to learn how to do good work, and to do it, is surely much greater when you know that the work has to be done, that it is going to be of real use to someone. (p. 121)

A few months have passed and my daughter is now 6 years old. Looking back, the journal writing initiative did not last very long and it was quickly superseded by her interest in writing emails to her friends and family and playing Scrabble. The medium has changed, but for her the process is very similar. She still consults others around her to ensure that she is spelling and using correct punctuation as she writes. She is also a prolific note writer. So she will send me messages that she has hand written, and either present them to me in an envelope or deliver the notes by hand or slide them under my door. When she wants to be secretive about the notes and it is only the two of us that are home, she does try to sound out words or spell as much of the word as she knows or guesses is correct and sometimes leaves the rest blank. The powerful point in all of this is that she is reading and writing authentically, organically, and meaningfully, and she is in control. She is not learning to spell arbitrary, disconnected words because some day she may make use of them, but she is spelling words for real reasons.

Some people may argue that, once again, there are many examples in formal schooling where students are spelling words for authentic reasons, such as journal responses. I question whether it is truly authentic, given that students are often forced to write. Some argue that I need to fashion the argument around how the language arts curriculum teaches spelling by using tests and spelling bees, for example. They suggest that it is a very deductive approach to learning; in other words, learn how to spell, and then you might need some of the words on the test when writing a journal response. However, in my mind a mandated journal is not the same as the meaningful, purposeful decisions Karina makes in writing her notes, emails, and so on. As well, for me this type of "just in case learning" does not seem to be authentic, genuine, and immediate. So learning to spell just in case one day you need to spell that word is not the same as learning to spell because you need to write something meaningful now. Despite, some still argue that the focus should be on the journal response first and foremost and that a version of what I am taking about was done back in the early 1990s with whole language, where students were encouraged to use whatever word they wanted to use, regardless of the spelling, in an attempt to foster creativity. However, parents jumped all over it and it was basically removed from the curriculum. Hence, they conclude that there have been elements within formal schooling that have used unschooling techniques, but they have been shot down. But this position misinterprets what unschooling is all about. Unschooling is not about whole language, but authentic, organic, and learner-centered democratic approaches. It is not about someone else creating a program, but it is about listening to the learner.

After reading a draft of this book, Pat Farenga informed me that Holt thought that Ken and Yetta Goodman's work was outstanding; Farenga also thought that the issue raised in the above paragraph is very important stuff.

Another thing we do from time to time is make up and play word games. The girls often make up the games and initiate the game playing. For example, Annabel made up a game where we would share the first letter of a word and how many letters the word contains. So for example, I would say the word has four letters and starts with "P." They would then guess, and if they did not guess correctly, the next letter would be supplied. So, I would say the next letter is "o" and so on until they guessed the word Pool. They even named the different games they make up so that we can easily know which game we are going to be playing. Again, the point is not to learn to spell words, but we spell words to play the game. I think this is a subtle, but important distinction. No one is ever forced to play, and we may go months and months never playing any of these games. When it happens it is a spontaneous desire that they have. We could be sitting on a beach relaxing, or in an airport waiting for our flight, or anywhere really.

This brings us to another of Farenga's points: that unschooling builds family unity. I just love when I see and hear my daughter approaching me with her journal in hand, a book, a note, a game, or whatever else. I know that it is another opportunity for us to cuddle and spend time close to each other. We often lie together with her next to me as she writes, all the while the bonding and the love flowing through us, leaving its indelible mark, just like the ink does to the page. The depth of our relationship becomes imprinted on our very being.

Admittedly, this enthusiasm is difficult to muster at times. When this happens, I merely explain that I am sorry, but I am tired or busy, and because they know that I would never refuse their advances unless I was truly in need of rest or some personal time, they fully understand. I am very fortunate this way. Being human we all have lapses, and we all need personal time. I show them the same respect when they need their time or when they are busy, and so they know from experience what I am feeling and how they should act. Modeling is a powerful tool.

Not only is modeling useful in moral and ethical situations, but it is also useful in more academic learning situations. Accordingly, at times, I may not know how a word is spelled, and I then have to model behavior for her, as Farenga points out. Being a model for young people and showing them what we do when we want to learn about something is of utmost value to a person who is trying to navigate the world of learning and trying to discover what resources we have at hand. This does not have to be an artificial attempt, but arises naturally as we get confronted with questions and needs that we cannot immediately answer or respond to. In my life I am constantly confronted with things that I have to research, and they witness this. Whether it is gardening information, or cooking, or chores, or words that I have to look up, I am always learning and researching. I consult friends, relatives, computers, and whatever resource I deem necessary to learn what I need to learn, when the needs arise. The wider we cast our net, the more resources we tap into and try to appeal to, the greater service we are providing for our young people. We can look online, but we can also go out into our community and tap into the riches that are there. And, of course, we need to ensure that modeling moves beyond mere mimicry and allow for imagination and creativity to soar. In other words, we want people to imagine and create a better world and not merely replicate what the world is like. Let's now turn to Rolstad.

When I asked Rolstad (2010, September 9) about the strength of unschooling she said,

The strengths are just tremendous. I think the biggest one is that it is just a completely customized experience. Everybody makes their own life, makes their own learning . . . I think for me the strengths of unschooling are, that's the big one, that it's just each person doing their own thing, authoring their own life, but without a script.

Rolstad echoes what the others have said about the importance of the customized experience of unschooling. Unschoolers can discover for themselves and build on their strengths and interests, if they so choose. Again, I take her statement that they do this without a script to mean that they do not have to follow an externally imposed curriculum or script, and that they can follow their own passions in developing and creating their script for themselves. I mention this again because many, I believe, mistakenly say that there is no curriculum in unschooling. I think this is inaccurate because I see curriculum in a much broader context. So I would say that perhaps there is not always an externally imposed curriculum, but there clearly is a curriculum that emerges. It may be flexible, subject to change, emerging, but there is a curriculum, a willed curriculum. By just being aware of what they've done, what they might explore, and what they want to discover next, unschoolers have a curriculum that is not just flexible, but one that has method and rational elegance as well. As Mintz suggests below, the outcome is not predetermined, and in that sense there may not always be a script.

Jerry Mintz (2010, September 9) says of the strengths of unschooling that

> I think that that's inherent in the idea that kids are natural learners. The potential is exponential. Anything can happen if you are working and building on the interest of the learner. Whereas what happens in the other paradigm is the outcome is predetermined and usually pretty mundane.

When we see learning as natural and we give people learner-centered democratic spaces to explore, it becomes clear that the potential is exponential. Rather than predetermining a script that everyone needs to follow, unschooling allows for richer, broader, and deeper learning. People can choose and follow their passions, rather than someone else's narrow, externally imposed ideas about what matters. Moreover, different things will matter for different people, and for the same person at different times. Perhaps the most passionate response comes from Davis because he is the most recent graduate of mainstream schooling and his wounds are very fresh. His response below makes this clear.

Mathew Davis (2010, September 10) articulates that the strength of unschooling is

> the self-determination. You're in control, you have to be self-disciplined. You learn so much more, you learn so much more than being in some machine that's set up for you to do this or set up for you to do that. You actually learn to be yourself, you have a sense of identity. That's the beauty of it and that's the strongest part of it, is the self-determination, because then you are focused and you do not have these other things, all these other hindrances and things like that to hold you back from what you really want to do. You don't have to play the game or work within the context of something that is inherently set up to make you a robot.

Having just come off of an externally imposed mainstream school experience, the notion of self-determination is very real for Davis as I read his response. He refers to mainstream schooling as a machine that has been designed to control what you do, that is designed to turn you into a robot. In contrast, he argues that unschooling allows you to focus on who you are and what you want to do and be. Unschooling allows you to remain in touch with yourself rather than insisting that you be someone else. Again, as I read Davis's words, I feel the pain and the wounds that he is now struggling to heal. I hear his confidence and his deep understanding of how he was viewed and how he views the system. He sees schooling for what it did to him, and not as a force for freedom and liberation, but a force of control and an obstacle, a hindrance.

In sum, the strengths of unschooling are that you can in fact investigate yourself, your neighborhood, the history that appeals to you, and you can figure out what parts of it you want to reproduce in your unschooling experience. You can in fact teach the way children learn, and it allows the most natural organic processes of our development to thrive and to have space to grow. It recognizes that people learn in different ways, at different paces, and for different reasons. It allows people to pursue the rhythm that is most natural to them, and unschooling is a way of releasing our natural potentials. Furthermore, it is tailored to the person's ability, the learner is a willing one, the learner gets to discover what he or she is interested in learning about, it brings families together, and allows for learning and living to be modeled. In short, it is a completely customized experience that is learner-centered and democratic. The learner needs to remain in control. It is the learning and the curriculum that both need to be customized. There are many examples of what appears to be customized learning in formal education, and that's why Gardner's Multiple Intelligence Theory gets so much attention in Bachelor of Education Programs, not to mention Individual Education Plans (IEPs) and other special education approaches. Of course, there are those like Kincheloe (2004) who, I think rightly, challenge Gardener's work. However, these mainstream examples do not mean that these experiences are necessarily authentic; still, they may qualify as customized to some extent. Everybody makes his or her own life, makes his or her own learning, and the potential is exponentially powerful. By unschooling, you learn so much more. Later on in the book I will say more about how unschooling's strengths are love, trust, respect, care, and compassion. Next we need to see what some of the perceived limitations of unschooling are so that we can do our best to try to avoid or mitigate them.

Again, I think that it is important to listen to others' thoughts on unschooling; especially those that have thought about it deeply and those that have a connection with what it is. For this reason, sharing Gatto's, Miller's, Farenga's, Mintz's, Rolstad's, and Davis's thoughts and responses on how they would define unschooling and what they see as its strengths and limitations is invaluable. These thinkers' ideas and variety of perspectives have helped me better understand unschooling. I continue to try to understand and to see where I fit in relation to the unschooling worldview. Of course, unschooling is not a homogeneous idea, and unschoolers are not a homogeneous group. They differ, and so by helping people better understand the philosophy and how it can play a part in our lives, we can better take full advantage of what unschooling has to offer.

4 LIMITATIONS OF UNSCHOOLING

Now that we have looked at how some prominent thinkers define unschooling, and we have looked at what the strengths of unschooling are, it is worthwhile to examine what some of the limitations or cautions are. Looking at the limitations will better prepare us to move forward, learning from what others caution us against. In speaking of limitations Gatto (2010b, September 9) cautions that

> if you become a total purist at unschooling and your own will occupies all your time, you're prone, it's not certain this will happen, but you are prone to emerge unbalanced because while you have energy and the insight and mental agility of being young, you unfortunately lack the experience with both the world and with history to make your judgments the best you're capable of. You tend to be moved by great enthusiasm that eats up all your time in one area or another area and it genuinely helps to have advice from people you trust, not from strangers.

I think that Gatto raises an important caution and one that, if you are aware, you can easily avoid falling victim to. Now it is important to note that Gatto does not argue that becoming unbalanced is an inevitable result of allowing your own will to occupy all of your time, nor is he arguing that all unschoolers allow their own will to occupy all of their time, but that it may happen and that, if it does, you may be prone to emerge unbalanced. I think that what is required is to look at your specific case and to understand that this may be a danger and something that you can become prone to, and then to evaluate your situation along with people you trust and see what steps you need to take, if any. Of course, focusing on yourself and ignoring others and your community is something that we all need to be cautious about, but all of us, regardless of whether we are unschoolers or not, should think about connecting with ourselves, our community, and other beings and nonbeings in our world. If we are interested in democracy and the overall well-being of our world, we need to be aware of how our actions impact our world. I think it might be worth pointing out that schooling often results in people who are unbalanced in MANY ways (emotionally, academically, spiritually, and bodily) and who are prone to ignore others, because schooling is individualistic and competitive. And increasingly, a hyper focus on academics at the exclusion of all else fuels the problem. Again, this is an important caution for unschoolers and schoolers alike. The balance between the individual and community in the broadest sense is crucial to improving the collective well-being, and in my experience I believe that this balance is routinely achieved by unschoolers.

At the same time, it is essential not to panic and not to be scared of a word like unbalanced. Being unbalanced can mean many things, and so it may be worthwhile to think of a few representative scenarios and to see how being unbalanced may not be something that we need to fear. In terms of achievement, some may fear that unbalanced means that someone who is not focusing on what mainstream schooling promotes is being unbalanced because they are focusing too much energy on their will. I would argue that in many cases focusing on your will and narrowing your focus is not a bad thing, and that can be determined only by each individual's unique life story. There is not an easy answer, nor is there a formula that we can universally apply algorithmically that will fit to every situation. Growing up and learning is an art, and so we must paint the canvas of our lives in masterful and personal ways. We must look at our own context and our own situation and make these types of determinations for ourselves. For example, I recently went to watch *Never say Never* (Chu, 2011), with my family and we thoroughly enjoyed the Justin Bieber documentary. There was one moment in the film, however, where Bieber is shown momentarily with chemistry and biology textbooks. Now, Bieber may have a genuine interest in these subjects and texts, and if he does that is fine and I wish him well in pursuing his interests. However, if they are exposing Bieber to biology and chemistry because others his age and in mainstream schooling are forced to study these disciplines, then I think we have clearly gone too far in fearing that Bieber will somehow become unbalanced because he lacks exposure to chemistry and biology. There is a lot to be said for someone who has a passion and follows his or her will. This applies to all of us and not just to stars or the exceptionally talented. Consequently, if this is what we mean by unbalanced, then being unbalanced may be a laudable end. The Justin Bieber example can also be an attempt to show the public that he is a regular kid who studies in school, rather than a mega pop star who does not attend school because he is making millions of dollars. It may therefore be about conformity. Thus, formal education may be rigid and inflexible, but it is also a symbol of conformity (not straying from the herd so to speak) that many within society find comforting.

By following a willed curriculum, inevitably you will connect with yourself and your world and grow accordingly. In the end, I believe that if you allow a learner-centered democratic approach to living that is based in love, respect, trust, care, and compassion as your guide, the danger that Gatto warns against will be minimal.

When asked about the limitations of unschooling R. Miller (2010) cautions:

There is a dilemma when we think of educational alternatives, there is always this balancing act between freedom and I guess you could call it structure. But it's recognizing that every individual is different and has personal styles and everything about us is unique, and yet we are also part of society. We are part of a larger world, we are part of an ecology, a natural world, and if we are only individualistic, if we only do what feels good to ourselves, I think we are missing something of the connection between the larger context that we live in. For unschoolers, I think, there is a danger [of] that, it's not a huge danger because people naturally want to connect, so I don't think most unschoolers just go off in their own little worlds and ignore the rest of the world, but I think it's something to be aware of if you're pursuing this path, that there are bigger issues, bigger problems, bigger challenges that we face as a species, as a community at whatever level you want to look at. We have responsibilities to a larger world, something outside of ourselves, and as long as you keep that in mind when you are unschooling you can have that balance, but that could be a danger if you lose sight of that. I think for most kids, most families, I wouldn't say that there are large drawbacks to unschooling, but there are probably many kids who do benefit from the social atmosphere of groups, of being in their neighbourhood school, for example. And I imagine there are some kids who might be missing out on certain experiences by unschooling. Most of the time that is probably compensated by other experiences that are probably healthier in their own ways, but it's probably not for everybody.

When Miller uses structure we can think of using the word constraint. In other words, having others structure a curriculum for us can be constraining, while self-structuring is a willed curriculum. Like Gatto, Miller's caution is critical and applies to all of us, whether we are unschooling or not. He cautions that unschoolers should strive to remain balanced, and that as an unschooler you understand that there is a larger world and that you need to be careful that you do not just go off into your own little world and ignore the rest of the world. Miller also reminds us of bigger challenges that we face as a species and as a community. I think his wisdom is worth heeding. In fact, for me unschooling holds so much promise because it allows people to spend time anywhere in the world, and in their communities, which will hopefully result in deeper connections to the places and spaces in which we spend time. Perhaps a large part of the disconnection that so many schooled people face is that they spend so much time enclosed in institutions and not enough time in the world at large. Therefore, if we are conscious and serious about what Miller suggests about the balance between the individual and community, then by unschooling we will be in a better position to avoid the pitfalls Miller warns against because we are unschooling.

Miller's point about the desire for young people to spend time in the social atmosphere of groups is one that I have noticed as well. Unfortunately, mainstream schooling has a monopoly on housing young people during the day, and so finding others in the local community with whom to interact is not always as easy as one would like. Of course, a social atmosphere of groups does not mean exclusively same-age peers. In fact, I believe that all people benefit from interacting in heterogeneous as well as homogeneous age groupings. Age segregation makes little sense, and so ensuring that unschoolers have plenty of opportunities to spend time with people of all ages results in a much more intelligent, emotional, and spiritually socialized person.

My children love to play with others and always have their friends over. Their friends are always welcome, and the more self-structured play and interactions my children experience the better, if that is what they will. Again, this is the case for my children and many other unschooling children that I know, but some may find less of a need for connecting and playing with others at different times in their lives. If they do find less of a need we should not panic and assume that there is a problem; similarly, if they have more of a need, it is also not in and of itself a problem. Again, we have to ultimately gauge the situation and the individual within a loving context and then make determinations based on that. I think that many people also go through stages and times in their lives where they prefer more company and at other times less. So in making any assumptions and decisions, it is best to focus long term and not short term and to look at the whole of someone's life rather than just specific situations.

As well, with the increasing numbers of homeschoolers and groups and events that are being organized that facilitate connections and gatherings of homeschoolers, this becomes less and less of an issue. In my community there are people gathering and events happening daily. In fact, there are so many events and gatherings that people have to pick and choose which among many they can fit into their schedules. Additionally, unschoolers and homeschoolers continually propose new events, activities, and gatherings to suit their needs and tastes, so there are always opportunities to create the spaces and places that you desire and to connect with other beings and the world.

With respect to limitations, Farenga (2010) says,

Limitations of unschooling are too much focus on the child. I think a really important thing is a balance between "being me and also us," to use a book I like from the 1980s by Alison Stallibrass. I've seen Matt Hern and Grace Llewellyn in interviews talk about it; in fact I think this is in print where they talk about it, they notice the current crop of unschoolers seem a little more self-centered than what they have had in the 1990s and they are not as involved in as many community activities, more introverted with computers, and me me me sort of stuff. So, I think those criticisms are valid, because if you are the center and you're having a self-directed learning experience that suddenly becomes completely child-centric around me and my interests and nothing else, that has benefits, but also has a danger of being selfish, and introverted, and just focused on yourself. So that's one of the dangers, that you really have to try and balance it by modeling behavior . . . but you need to make the effort; if you just think, I am going to unschool and they are going to follow whatever they want and whatever interests they have and I am just going to feed that and that's that, I think you are missing an important part of the picture, which is also that they need a social development that involves an outreach to a larger community besides the family; but first you start with the family, and then from there, it's a concentric circle, with your local community and then your community, and outside that perhaps college, moving away, and travel. I think travel is a really important thing, a strength of unschooling that a lot of families do take advantage of and one of the strengths of unschooling and homeschooling overall . . . . all of this is a way of saying that if you are not aware of the larger world and where your child and you fit in the larger world, you do run the danger of becoming too insular with unschooling.

Again, I think this applies to us all, and perhaps the fact that Hern and Llewellyn see the children they meet as being more me-centered, this could be a trend that goes beyond unschooling, or it could be Hern and Llewellyn looking at young people from a more mature stage in their life. I point this out simply to suggest that what is being suggested about young people being more me-centered may be more nuanced than first appears, yet it is something that I agree we need to be aware of.

One promising trend that you may have noticed so far is that Gatto, Miller, and Farenga are all cautioning about similar limitations. This is encouraging because, had they all been outlining different limitations, then unschooling may be less appealing since there would be so much to consider. However, because the limitations shared are very similar, then there is less to be concerned about when unschooling. As long as we ensure that there is a balance between "being me and also us," as Farenga quotes Stallibrass, then we can feel very comfortable that we are mitigating a potential danger that many may fear. Again, if we think of unschooling not as something that limits our options but as something that understands that the world and everything in it is a potential teacher and a potential student, and that we have to respect ourselves and other beings and things, then looking after ourselves, others, and the world will flow naturally. As long as we do not become insular, as Farenga says, then we are fully taking advantage of being with the world and with communities of all sorts. I think it's worth pointing out here that there is no way to "ensure" any of this. We can't do anything to ensure that unschoolers take this or that attitude; we can only encourage thinking and dialogue. But institutionalizing children doesn't ensure anything either. They may become selfish and insular by being schooled.

If we consider many of the advocates of unschooling and their life histories, we will notice that they are caring, compassionate, trusting, respectful, and loving people who spend a lot of time working for others and the larger world. Therefore, it makes perfect sense that people who are so committed to their world and the beings in it would urge unschoolers, and all of us for that matter, to share the same laudable goals. In addition, it makes sense that given how committed and passionate unschooling advocates are to bettering the world, they would be drawn to a philosophy, worldview, and a way of life that's equally committed because of how it reflects their life stories. So, to assume that unschooling is philosophically prone to making people insular makes little sense, given that so many unschooling advocates and unschoolers are not inward looking or narrow-minded. Nevertheless, I think the caution is a worthwhile reminder for us all that the best way to prepare for the adult world is to engage with it, play with it, and embrace the parts of it that resonate most with us, and that through love, trust, respect, care, and compassion, good will follow.

Of the limitations Mintz (2010) says,

I think that kids who are raised as unschoolers are very, very dangerous to the system [laughs]. They will perhaps overturn the boat . . . . but seriously, I think that this is why we probably don't have a whole society of people like that because with so many dynamic people, it means a very dynamic balance has to be created, and I think that when that happens, I think we go into a whole new realm.

Although somewhat tongue in cheek, Mintz's caution is actually something that everyone who takes democracy seriously should embrace rather than be concerned about. In a democracy we should value diversity and confidence and people who are willing to challenge people and policies that need to be challenged. We all grow and are better off for having people like that, especially those that are interested in making the world a better place by making it less racist, less sexist, less homophobic, less classist, less ageist, less destructive, and so on.

It is clear to me that mainstream schooling does not encourage people to challenge, but instead focuses on obedience. For the most part, many would agree with my statement about mainstream schooling, but some might suggest that they have also had many teachers in the past that cultivated a classroom where challenging the teacher and the status quo was expected. However, ultimately, the rules of schooling such as requiring marks and the undemocratic systemic culture of schooling always result in this possibility of challenging the status quo being diminished. This is evident in how schoolers and schooling advocates co-opt and subvert the meaning of important words, even words like respect. For a schooler, being respectful means that you must listen to and obey those in positions of power over you, like teachers and administrators. That you do not challenge, and that you accept and show respect to your elders because they are elders. So, things like doing your homework and following orders are signs of respect. To me, this is a very funny definition of respect that disempowers rather than empowers. Of my two daughters, one has decided to go to school and the other has decided not to at this point. I see my schooled daughter following orders and doing what she is asked to do and "respecting" others, unfortunately at the expense of respecting herself. She does what she does in her schooling day mostly because she has embodied the notion that out of respect for others you need to ignore your own interests and desires. She has little interest in much of what she does, and she does it because she is told and would never choose to do it if it was not imposed on her. I try to mitigate this by talking to her about it and by giving her a loving environment, where she is truly respected and trusted when she is with my wife, and me, and having said that, I do find it hard to witness what happens to her when she is in school. Again, attending school is a choice she has made, largely in order to be with her friends during the school day, and so I have to continue to support her in that decision. The schooling definition of respect is largely broken because it has lost a sense of balance. It is far too skewed in the direction of the "we" and has lost touch with the "me." It is about obedience to the other at the expense of the self. This skewing in the other direction shows the danger of schooling, namely, that children may lose themselves in their attempts to be part of the crowd.

Alfie Kohn (2011) has a piece with a great title that makes my point clearer. The title of the piece is "Challenging students—and how to have more of them." I think he is absolutely correct that if we are interested in democracy we need people who are willing to stand up and to challenge. Kohn shares how as a brand-new high school teacher he wore a button that read QUESTION AUTHORITY. "One girl," he wrote, "wanted to know who had appointed me the school's question authority" (p. 40). Of course she questioned the authority figure while doing it, but Kohn shares the story to make the point that she took the phrase as a descriptive label rather than an exhortation. He then goes on to share the following:

> This is essentially the same state of affairs that Norm Diamond, an Oregon educator and labor activist, was trying to capture when he invented a syndrome called Compliance Acquiescent Disorder (CAD). He intended it as a spoof of Oppositional Defiant Disorder (ODD), for which countless children are referred for treatment. A local newspaper ran an advertisement that itemized symptoms of ODD ("argues with adults," "actively defies rules") and invited parents who thought they had such children to allow them to be given an experimental medication. In response, Diamond placed a counter-ad about CAD in the paper. An individual with this disorder, it explained, "defers to authority," "actively obeys rules," "fails to argue back," "knuckles under instead of

mobilizing others in support," "stays restrained when outrage is warranted," and so on. (pp. 40–41)

Philosophically, unschooling encourages us to question and to challenge. Perhaps by questioning and challenging we may change someone else's position or we may change our position, or perhaps both will occur. What will happen is not clear, but what is clear is that a healthy democracy demands this, and an unhealthy democracy (if this can even be called a democracy) makes this very difficult to do.

I have purposely placed Rolstad's and Davis's responses to the limitations of unschooling together because they speak to each other. Even though the one did not hear the other's response to the question before responding themselves, the responses work well together. For Rolstad (2010, September 9) she cautions about the limitations of unschooling by sharing the following:

> I think it's a little bit like asking what are the limitations of having kids. Anything in the negative that comes to mind you think that it's just in the nature of it and you know when people ask, for example, what about poor or minority kids, how can they unschool? I think that reflects prejudice, and I think that it's a lack of respect for the knowledge. In language minority education, which is something I know a lot about, I worked with that for a long time, we talk about funds of knowledge, this idea that this family, every family, every culture, has these funds of knowledge that school either taps or doesn't tap, and so I think the same thing goes with unschooling. You can tap any kind of knowledge, any kind of cultural wisdom or family practices or knowledge, so I don't think that unschooling can be ruled out for anybody, not that it's for everybody automatically. People who don't want to do it, of course, shouldn't be unschooling. The other one that people will talk about is for social justice. School people are sure that everyone has to be shown how to be taught to be tolerant of diversity. I think that schools do a terrible job of that, and I also think that when you trust and respect children they naturally value other people and it's easy for them to just

turn to somebody new and think, okay this is how you treat somebody with honor, respect, and dignity. I think that kids who are oppressed and bullied the way they are in schools just naturally look for other people to pick on and any weakness or any reason to differentiate themselves from others. It's like a balance, it's really a balance, and I think what schools offer is not at all a balance. And I think that unschooling offers much more of a balance, and I think that balance is something you can't give to somebody else. Children find balance, they do that themselves. You can support them. A brand new baby, you have to take care of them, you have to help them find their balance, but more and more that balance shifts away from the parent to the child. I sometimes think about Jerome Bruner who said in the 1960s that instruction is all about making a person self-sufficient, and I think that babies are born self-sufficient, cognitively self-sufficient. We help their bodies, we help them eat and live physically, but I think they are cognitively self-sufficient. They know what they need to do to learn what they need to learn . . . . I think it's important to trust children to do what they are already capable and competent to do.

And when asked about the limitations Davis responded,

Of course, of course. Unschooling is not for everyone, let's make that clear also. I can never unschool as it is right now. The way things are right now, most minorities cannot unschool, poor people cannot unschool. And of course there is something wrong with that, but I am not saying that unschooling is bad. I am just saying it works for some people and other people it won't work. And I don't want people to work under the assumption that it works for everyone, because that's not the case. But for the people who it does work for, I think it's beautiful.

I then followed up by asking why he thinks it would not work for certain groups. He said,

For example, minority and poor people, and I am one. I am a minority and I grew up in poverty. So we have to learn a

THE WILLED CURRICULUM, UNSCHOOLING, AND SELF-DIRECTION

certain language of power. So, for example, if I go to India I have to learn the language. I have to learn the customs, the beliefs, the traditions in order to survive in that culture. So, it's the same thing for minorities and poor people in America because we live in a White power structure, so we have to learn to work through that language of power, and the only way we are going to get that is through formal skills, is through . . . getting those formal skills in the system, or if not, getting something to that equivalent outside of the system in a school, it has to be an institution almost. I am not saying that it is the end all and be all, but I am just saying that that is something that holds poor people and minorities back from unschooling. Now am I saying that that is the case for all minorities and poor people?—no. I am sure that some people can, but not everybody.

Funny that Davis says this since, as I mentioned before, what little I know about him after hearing him speak about his life and his lack of achievement in school, it seems that he has been unschooling while attending school. He has been unschooling himself in what matters to him and in what he values while playing the survival game of school. For example, he shares how his teachers discounted him and his school work, and that they were not even aware of what he was doing outside of schooling.

In the end he does recognize that what he is suggesting does not apply to all poor and minorities and to suggest that it will not work for all poor and minority people is unfair. I assume he would ultimately agree with Rolstad when she says that unschooling cannot be ruled out for anybody. She also acknowledges that it may not be for everyone automatically, and that for people who choose not to unschool, then unschooling is not for them. Finally, what Rolstad says above really and truly resonated with me, and I think it is worthwhile rewriting it and allowing it to stand on its own: "and I also think that when you trust and respect children they naturally value other people and it's easy for them to just turn to somebody new and think, okay this is how you treat somebody with honor, respect, and dignity."

I think these words are beautiful and a powerful reminder of how positive and gentle childrearing can and should be.

5 LOVE AND THE WILLED CURRICULUM

Love is the most overused term that is underused. The previous sentence may not make sense, but what I am trying to capture by using it is that on the one hand, you can barely have a conversation with someone without the word love being used. For example, people talk about loving ice-cream and movies and so on. On the other hand, where it matters most, the word love is barely referenced. For example, among educators, who ought to be tightly focused on the loving care and nurturing of children as they grow into happy, well-adjusted adults, the word love is barely referenced. The word is often overused in trivial ways and underused when it comes to substantive issues. When it comes to the willed curriculum, this is not the case. In fact, the word love surrounds, is linked, and is intertwined with the willed curriculum. At its most basic element the term love can replace the willed curriculum and still make a lot of sense. What is so beautiful about the willed curriculum is that it is, among other things, love in action.

In a discussion about love, I think it is useful to start with how love has traditionally been thought about. Borrowing from the work of Christopher Phillips (*Socrates in Love*, 2007), John P. Miller (2010) discusses six forms of love, adding self-love to the five forms of love described by Phillips. First, Miller writes about self-love, love of family, love of friends, love of strangers, agape, and eros (p. 83). Miller says that self-love needs to begin with ourselves; that we need to love ourselves before we can love others (p. 83). Second, he writes that love of family is a natural and spontaneous form of love (p. 84). Third, love of friends also is what binds together communities (p. 86). Fourth, love of strangers was inspired by the Greeks and served to ensure that if you needed a place to stay when you were off somewhere, you could count on strangers to house you and in turn you were expected to do the same (p. 87). Fifth, agape is love with no expectation of reciprocity (p. 89). And sixth, eros is universal love that goes beyond the individual (p. 90).

Of course, love is so central and integral a concept that it can and does apply to everything, and love is central to the understanding of the willed curriculum. In what follows, I will talk about love and how it connects to the willed curriculum in a more pedestrian way. I will share personal observations about love and how it is central and intricately linked to unschooling and thereby the willed curriculum. Without love the willed curriculum cannot be. The willed curriculum and love are intertwined like a mobius strip. Love is at the center and drives and controls the willed curriculum. Without love the willed curriculum becomes an externally driven, externally imposed chore. When something is done with love, whatever that something is, it takes us to a whole new realm. For example, think about what it means to do simple tasks like that of washing dishes as a chore versus washing dishes with love. Clearly, when dishwashing is done with love, the level of engagement and mindfulness that is associated from the experience becomes something infinitely more meaningful and beautiful than merely the chore of washing dishes. It becomes divine, it becomes an experience of life itself, it becomes love, it becomes the willed curriculum in that the washer, like the learner, is engaging with the activity in deep ways.

You may think that washing dishes as I describe it above is a silly example. I have taught at every level from kindergarten, to high school, to undergraduate, to graduate school. I have,

THE WILLED CURRICULUM, UNSCHOOLING, AND SELF-DIRECTION

unfortunately, been in a position where I felt compelled to force others to complete tasks that they would otherwise never choose to do. At the beginning of my formal teaching career within mainstream schooling, I used marks as a way to manipulate students to do what they otherwise would choose not to do. So, I have witnessed people firsthand, including myself, being wounded and doing things in a chore-like way and not out of love.

To extend the significance of this even further I will share what Thich Nhat Hanh (1987) says about washing the dishes:

> While washing the dishes one should only be washing the dishes, which means that while washing the dishes one should be completely aware of the fact that one is washing the dishes. At first glance this might seem a little silly: why put so much stress on a simple thing? But that's precisely the point. The fact that I am standing there and washing these bowls is a wondrous reality. I'm being completely myself, following my breath, conscious of my presence, and conscious of my thoughts and actions. There's no way I can be tossed around mindlessly like a bottle slapped here and there on the waves. (p. 6)

Hanh goes on to say that there are two ways to wash the dishes. The first way is to wash the dishes in order to have clean dishes, and the second way is to wash the dishes in order to wash the dishes. (p. 7)

> If while we are washing dishes, we think only of the cup of tea that awaits us, thus hurrying to get the dishes out of the way as if they were a nuisance, then we are not "washing the dishes to wash the dishes." What's more, we are not alive during the time we are washing the dishes . . . . If we can't wash the dishes, the chances are we won't be able to drink our tea either. (pp. 7–8)

As we can see, even a task as simple as washing the dishes can be a loving and mindful experience. By allowing learners the dignity of following their will, the possibility that things will be done with a mindful, loving flow increases.

Unfortunately, as a mainstream schoolteacher, I witnessed young people being broken, being molded, being oppressed, being forced to break away from themselves. I have played the role of prison guard and imposed my and other people's wills on people. As an unschooling parent, I have witnessed my daughters doing the exact same tasks that schoolers often engage in, not out of a sense of duty, but with love, and the difference is otherworldly. I can think of many remarkable examples, but now I am thinking of my 5-year-old daughter who just last night asked me to help her find the website that lets her add numbers. Children are asked to add numbers and do work sheets everyday, and for far too many, it becomes a chore since they have no choice in the matter. My daughter has done both, and the difference is that she chooses to do the tasks and they were not externally imposed on her. This is not a daily desire of hers, and she can go months or years never wanting to visit those activities again, and that is fine. There are many, many ways to develop literacy and numeracy (again, I use this as an example because so many are so obsessed with literacy and numeracy). There are no critical periods whereby after a particular date your ability to learn academic skills expires. Worden, Hinton, and Fischer (2011) explain how, "while there is evidence for limited critical periods in brain development in limited domains (such as the strength of vision in the two eyes), no evidence supports a critical period for academic skills" (p. 11). Ultimately, for many learners, when they are told when to learn, how to learn, for how long to learn, and then judged on what and how well they learned, their desire and love for learning diminishes. I know mine certainly does.

Many may be surprised that a young person is asking to do simple math problems out of love, but it is true. It happens, and it is a beautiful thing to witness. I know that if I ask her to do it when she is not in the mood to, it will become a chore and it will not be done with love. And that makes all the difference. The activity is not what matters, but love is. For example, if I ask my daughter to do one of her favorite things, no matter what that is, and she does not have the will to do it at that moment, then it becomes a chore. The interconnection between will and love matters.

Watching someone do something with love is watching someone in what Mihaly Csikszentmihalyi (1997) calls flow. Of flow he says, "Contrary to what happens all too often in everyday life, in moments such as these what we feel, what we wish, and what we think are in harmony" (p. 29).

As a teacher I can honestly say that I did not witness my students or other people's students doing things with love. And those that did appear to do things with love were often interested in the mark they would get and in the competiveness of the task, both of which are inconsistent with love. Even those who completed tasks with a semblance of love often would fail to do things with love because they were ultimately made to feel anxious about what others would think and how what they did would be judged or scored. Doing something with love is doing it for its own sake, doing it, as we say, for the love of it. This is where the word amateur comes from. The "ama" stands for "amare" which means love in Latin. In other words, amateurs do not get paid, they do it for the love of it.

As an example of the willed curriculum, unschooling and love go hand in hand because what motivates us to unschool is also rooted in love. The message that too often seeps into our cultural discourse is that children should be sent to school to give parents a break. I do not intend this as a judgmental statement but merely to point out that unschooling requires a different kind of commitment and sends a different message. In some cases it requires financial, career, personal, emotional, bodily, or spiritual sacrifices. Again, I am not being judgmental, but simply pointing out that in some cases unschooling requires an added commitment: the commitment to spend time with one's children. Others, of course, me included, have been able to make it work seamlessly within my life. I am fortunate enough to be able to work from home much of the time, to get help with child care, mostly from my parents when I need them, to offset my schedule with my wife's, and to take my unschooled 5-year-old daughter with me when possible. The latter has meant that she has attended and participated in several conferences, a remarkable experience for someone so young. To date this has worked out extremely well. Having said that, I am amazed at how committed and creative caregivers are in rearranging things, if needed, to ensure that they can unschool those they care deeply about. Those who unschool come from a range of demographics including single parents and people with a range of incomes, and they all find ways to make it work for them by relying on friends, families, creating cooperatives, and so on.

If we want young people to learn to love, we need to surround them with love, shower them with love, and model love. The willed curriculum is the premier manifestation of love. It is about accepting people for who they are, unconditionally. As Alfie Kohn (2005) says of unconditional love,

the second sort of love is *un*conditional [the first is conditional]: it doesn't hinge on how they act, whether they're successful or well behaved or anything else. I want to defend the idea of unconditional parenting on the basis of both value judgment and a prediction. The value judgment is, very simply, that children shouldn't have to earn our approval. We ought to love them, as my friend Deborah says, "for no good reason." Furthermore, what counts is not just that we believe we love them unconditionally, but that *they feel* loved in that way.

The prediction, meanwhile, is that loving children unconditionally will have a positive effect. It's the right thing to do, morally speaking, but also a smart thing to do. Children need to be loved as they are and for who they are. When that happens, they can accept themselves as fundamentally good people, even when they screw up or fall short. And with this basic need met, they're also freer to accept (and help) other people. Unconditional love, in short, is what children require in order to flourish. (Kohn, 2005, p. 11).

Although Kohn is more of a progressive educator along the lines of John Dewey than an advocate for unschooling, I believe that his description of unconditional parenting is worthwhile for unschoolers to consider. I think a lot of what Kohn says is easy for unschoolers to appreciate, and this description is a case in point. It is through love and unschooling that people, all people regardless of age, can unfold and create themselves. Of course, this does not mean that I am unaware of or ignoring external conditions that put pressure on what people can accomplish. For some, it is clearly more difficult than for others, and we must continue to challenge the unjust forces of racism, classism, ageism, and so on.

I use the terms unfold and create deliberately to make the point that I believe that nature and nurture work together and that the combination helps people reach or not reach their full potential. The notion of unfolding suggests that what we become is always already within, and with the proper environment this unfolding will happen. There is something to this, but there is also something to the concept that we create ourselves as well. In my mind these ideas work in harmony and work best when unfolding and self-creation work in a loving relationship with each other.

Of course there are cases where people who were forced to learn things as children share how they were glad, later in life, that this was the case. And there are those who at first do things as a chore and then report that they grew to love them. There is no doubt that this is the case in some instances, but I believe it is always more complicated. First, I think we need to ask at what cost or sacrifice to the person's Self did this happen? Second, we need to think about whether this person would have been just as successful if they had been allowed and supported to unfold and create themselves without coercion, perhaps in a different area. There is so much dissatisfaction and unhappiness among people in their daily work and life that we cannot help but ask how things would differ if people were encouraged to do things lovingly throughout their lives.

Many of us may find it hard to believe that people will pursue paths that we are revolted by. For example, those of us who are math phobic may find it difficult to understand and appreciate that there are people in the world who love math and that there are amateurs and hobbyists who cannot wait to do math, who spend enormous amounts of time doing it out of love. I know I was shocked when my then 4-year-old daughter declared that she loved math. Rather than directing everyone into the latest focus within schooling (STEM, for example: science, technology, engineering, and mathematics), what would happen if we encouraged love to be his or her guide? I believe that schools should encourage children to follow their hearts in choosing career paths rather than pushing all children onto the same path. Would worker dissatisfaction decrease? More important, should the focus on workers dictate how we raise children? In other words, should people be treated as cogs to be fit into the economic machine to satisfy an economic vision that has resulted in billions of people being unhappy at work, or should something else, love, for instance, be our guiding principle?

When my unschooled daughter was 5 years old, she and her schooled 5-year-old friend were making crafts and colouring. Partly from convention, and the necessity to distinguish one from the other, they signed them. My daughter signed hers "KARiNA" using a mix of capitals and lowercase letters, while her friend signed hers conventionally: "Xxxxx." Not long after this incident, my daughter began writing her name using proper capitalization. Even when writing emails and sentences she asks about when to use capitals and even punctuation. She figured these things out on her own time, at her own pace, I assume, largely by watching and observing the world. Perhaps she noticed her friend's model. If so, this would be a nice example of learning from peers naturally, which school often makes unnecessarily difficult. Although remnants of this are still possible in formal schooling, it does not happen often enough and its possibility is diminished by the way schools are set up in large part because it is imposed and artificial and not willed, natural. The ability to do this is another advantage of the willed curriculum and a great skill to hone. These conventions are not difficult for most people to grasp, when they are ready to. Again, when my daughter writes for other audiences, she wants to make sure that she is following proper conventions, and so she asks and uses whatever human resources are available to her to ensure that she is conforming to writing conventions. Children want to participate in the adult world as well as create whole new languages and forms of writing, and so wanting to understand adult conventions is not a chore but a desire. In other words, children LOVE to make up codes, languages, secret messages . . . but they also want to learn and use the standard ways of writing and speaking, of course. So learning adult conventions is a desire, not a chore, unless and until teachers or other adults strip away children's desire to learn.

It becomes a chore only if coercion is employed instead of freedom. Having said that, the reason I share the above story is that when I saw the signed works, I felt compelled to point out to my already aware daughter that the way she spelled her name was against convention; in other words, she should spell it "Karina" not "KARiNA." That damn devil teacher in me! But my devil teaching differs from the mainstream teaching in powerful ways, in that I do not manipulate through testing and grading, which I believe makes a huge difference.

At the 7th annual AERO conference, I attended Pat Farenga's (2010) talk. In it he shared a story about John Holt (which I hope that I am repeating correctly) where Holt had felt compelled to correct/advise a young person on their work, and then he entered into an office where Farenga was and was rueful and disappointed in himself. Plus, he was making a joke by saying "The devil teacher made me do it." It is a reference to Flip Wilson, a popular 1970s comedian, whose character Geraldine would get in trouble and justify it by saying, "The devil made me do it." The idea is that we need to avoid imposing on others the devil teacher we all have within, in favor of a more gentle one that has a better understanding and capacity to work with learners rather than work on them. The "devil teacher" is a style of teacher that is very controlling and wants to correct everything. Some may argue that they have known many teachers in conventional schooling that are not "devil teachers." Although this may be the case, the problem of schooling goes beyond the notion of the devil teacher.

At the end of the day, I know that what I did was unnecessary and perhaps irritating to Karina. I know she knows how to write her letters and knows the difference between capital letters and lowercase. I have seen her use both appropriately. If we are not allowed freedom of expression even in writing our own names, what freedom do we have?" e. e. cummings and bell hooks famously do not conform.

Some may argue that I did the right thing in that I need to ensure that she conforms so that she develops good habits. This argument does not resonate with me. I am thinking of clothing as an example. Most of the time, I wear casual and comfortable clothing. That is my habit, but if I am going to a formal event I know and conform by wearing the conventional proper attire. In my case, I sacrifice comfort and don a noose around my neck, otherwise known as a tie. I sport a jacket that always seems to feel constricting no matter how expensive and impressive the designer label.

Admittedly, as soon as I make my entrance I loosen my tie and remove my jacket, as I watch the many others struggle to reach for things because they refuse to take off their jackets for fear of breaking convention, perhaps.

Before you judge me too unfairly, I am not alone. I have witnessed people wearing uncomfortable shoes and sharing tales about how much damage their shoes are doing to their feet. In fact, recently a friend teetered toward me, as if drunk and in pain at the same time, sharing how she was walking funny and she knew it, but it was because of the shoes that she was just not used to wearing. Having said that, my daughters love to dress up. This speaks to difference and diversity that needs to be respected. In my case, sometimes I choose to conform, as we all must at times, but many times this is not the case. At times we do have to sacrifice the "me" for the "us," and when to do so and when to agree to stand aside is an ongoing negotiation of which we ultimately have to maintain control. When I say "we," I mean everyone, not just parents.

In terms of spelling and punctuation, I am aware that it is just a matter of convention and, just like clothing, I and others can easily switch between formal, conventionally correct and informal, conventionally incorrect. When I write notes or shopping lists, I rarely bother with convention. I switch from cursive, to printing, to upper-, to lowercase, and sometimes what appears to be Sanskrit to others but is in fact merely my sloppy writing. In fact, even when I send emails, for the sake of speed mostly, I usually forgo the need for capitalization and just type.

I think of e. e. cummings and bell hooks, whose use of small letters reminds me that writing style, like any semiotic system, is political, that writing is not neutral, but is an externally imposed convention that has taken on almost fundamentalist religious status, and that writing-style debates remain contentious.

Even more to the point, when I look around at the world, I notice that in many cases these conventions are not adhered to. Many of the newspapers and magazines and products that have words splattered on them are for all intents and purposes "incorrect." Look around and see what I mean. Letters in words are all capitalized, or all lowercase, or a random combination, and in some cases, in the wrong, unconventional order—think of the infamous iProducts. Personally, I have no problem with all of this and actually applaud it.

For those who argue that "you can't break the rules until you know them," first, I would suggest that in this case the rules need to be rethought since there are so many exceptions to them, so what are the rules anyway? As well, if there are rules that are necessary, then we need to trust that when the need arises the rules will be internalized or assistance sought. I am thinking here of my older daughter who is now 8 and in the midst of writing a novel. She has just completed her first two chapters, and she has asked me to read it and comment. It was clear that the content was great, but the format needed to be edited. We sat together and we went through it together. She understands that format and conventions are important, and so she is asking someone whom she believes can help her, to help her. Similarly, when people submit to the peer review journal that I founded and edit, their work often needs to be proofread. In the same way, my work also benefits from proofreading and comments by others. So when the time comes, we can seek assistance from others and/or we can learn what needs to be done at the appropriate time, and that will be different for different people and contexts.

All of this is to say that we should relax and allow all the KARiNAs of the world to spell their names as they see fit. There is a time and a place for correct conventions, and correcting and prodding and directing and ultimately turning off young people from the joy of writing is not the way to proceed. Let's all bury the "devil teacher" within and allow creativity, imagination, and joy to flourish. When the time is right, when a person decides a convention is important and worth learning, conventions can easily be learned and adhered to. Yes, there is a time and a place for using conventional forms, but that doesn't mean conventional forms must ALWAYS be used, and it is not worth sacrificing joy by forcing and imposing rigid standards when they are not wanted or asked for. For example, with respect to writing, introducing too many corrections often results in frustration and lack of enjoyment, a result most of us would not approve of. In the end, it's a fine balance that should be sought out by learners, not imposed. That balance has moved too far away from the needs and wants of the learner and toward an external inflexible standard.

Out of curiosity, I recently perused a few of the curriculum documents in Ontario at the elementary and secondary levels. The documents are about 150–270 pages in length and, of the 10 I reviewed, some contained the term "love" within the documents, albeit only two, three, or four times within each and in very similar contexts. For example, one of the most recent documents to be released (it is so new that it is still listed in draft form) is the *Full-Day Early Learning Kindergarten Program 2010–*

2011. The document lists the term "love" in the following sentences:

> The Early Learning–Kindergarten team plays a critical role in fostering a positive attitude towards mathematics by valuing a child's early attempts at problem solving, by sharing and celebrating the child's learning, and by encouraging in each child a love of mathematics. (Ontario Ministry of education, 2010–2011, p. 20)

And,

> The school library program supports success by encouraging children to read and use many forms of text for understanding and enjoyment, and helping them to gather and use information effectively. The school library program enables children to: develop a love of reading for learning and for pleasure. (p. 46)

And,

> The personal and social development of young children lays the social and cognitive groundwork that fosters a love for school, engages the children in the process of learning, and supports future success in school and in life. (p. 50)

My understanding of love is very different from how love is used here. To me love is largely ineffable and is something that comes from within. To me, when someone imposes something on you in very direct ways, I think that it hinders love. We cannot make people love things; we cannot create a curriculum that will manipulate people into loving things. There is no recipe that will lead to a class of approximately 26 people loving mathematics, reading, and school.

Just as important as it is to love other things and beings, we have to love ourselves. And by loving and being loved we learn to love ourselves. By loving ourselves we learn to respect our bodies, minds, spirits, and emotions. We learn to treat ourselves with love, and love guides us to protect ourselves from harm; love excites and encourages us to pursue our dreams and reach our potential. Unfortunately, we see far too many people who do not love themselves, who destroy their bodies, minds, emotions, and spirits because they lack love of self. We need to ask ourselves why so many young people are inflicting so many wounds on themselves and what we as a society can do to stop the pain and help people heal. There is no doubt in my mind that love is a big part of the answer, and so we must do all that we can to increase love of self, and any system or society that diminishes love of self needs to review what they can do to ensure that the trend is reversed. This is made more difficult because defining love is difficult; it is perhaps the most imprecise word due to its many connotations and implications.

In a recent newspaper article, Brown (2011) draws our attention to the stress that young people are under. She writes, "They come to the guidance counselor with headaches and tears and insomnia and nerves and grades dragged down by the expectations that weigh on their teenaged shoulders." She goes on to share that there is a "growing number of students diagnosed with clinical depression and anxiety disorders — and more who seem headed that way, especially in Grade 9." In fact she quotes David Johnston, the Centre for Addiction and Mental Health board's senior manager of professional support services, who states, "The latest study by CAMH showed 36 per cent of Ontario students feel stress, which is concerning, if not alarming." So, given this alarm, what is their solution? The solution is "to run a week of lunchtime workshops in meditation, laughter therapy, dance, tai chi, and the 'sound escape' of listening to music played on crystals." The reason I raise this is that, to me, it is unconscionable that young people are suffering, and rather than dealing with the sources and causes of suffering, they appear to blame the individuals, and try to give them mechanisms to cope rather than transform and eliminate the problems that are causing anxiety and depression. Now, I have nothing against these strategies, and, in fact, I believe that they are worthwhile, but they should not be used to mask the real problems. The things that are directly causing the anxiety and depression need to change, not the individuals. This is a clear example of how we have lost sight of what really matters and how we are willing to sacrifice individuals for the sake of an externally imposed curriculum.

In conclusion, love is as much about the collective as it is about the individual. If we truly embrace love, we understand the importance of the collective "we." We understand that the collective assists in our nurturance and growth, while at the same time we nurture the collective and help it grow. We understand that we are a part of the world, and by making the immediate world we live in more loving, we are making our whole world more loving. Love is about being concerned for how our actions impact others as well as ourselves.

In the end, to truly embrace love, we need to trust, which is the subject of the next chapter.

6 TRUST AND THE WILLED CURRICULUM

It is clear to me that we do not trust young people, and it is even clearer to me that we should. To many of us, love and trust go hand in hand, and so if we want to take self-directed learning seriously, we need to trust young people. Unfortunately, scarcely a day goes by when I do not witness young people being treated as if they cannot be trusted. Young people are not allowed to make their own decisions, even with things that are intimate and personal to their own well-being, and even with things that only they can know.

I see children being force-fed, force-dressed, and force-schooled. Young people are not trusted to make decisions for themselves. How can this help a person's development? How can force-feeding, for example, be a positive thing? How can someone external to the person's body be a better judge of what the person should eat than the person herself? If a person is hungry or not, only that person can know. We need to learn to trust our children and to trust our own bodies, minds, emotions, and spirits. I believe that our bodies are sophisticated enough to be able to know what we need, what feels right when we eat it, and what feels wrong when we eat it. A 50-year-old shared with me how his father had forced him to eat seafood when he was a child. His father assumed that his protest at not wanting to eat seafood was a result of a young child being defiant and stubborn.

Hence, the battles around eating seafood were hard fought, and it was not until years later that he was officially diagnosed with a serious seafood allergy. To this day, if he is at a party he needs to leave the room when fish is served because he reacts to even the smell of seafood. His body knew what his parent could never know.

The same applies with being full. This is something that only the being can determine. Only they can know if they need more food. In fact, I believe that the reason so many are unhealthy and obese is because we have been raised not to listen to our internal guides but to listen to an external authority or message that forces us to eat, to finish everything on our plates whether we want it or not. We are taught to overeat and to not trust ourselves.

Whether the issue is what to eat or how much to eat, I believe that children need to be trusted. Perhaps a few examples will help to make my argument clearer. When our daughters were very young, my wife and I realized that we should trust our children to decide what it is they should eat. So, our daughters get to decide what they want to eat, and we make a wide variety of foods available to them. In all honesty, I believe that my daughters eat a healthier diet than I do. Even I am surprised at how well they eat. With the choice to eat whatever they want, including the treats that are readily available in our treat cupboard, they still manage to eat a healthy diet.

Along these lines, I recall a story about a girl who was around 2 years old at the time. She was not going to the bathroom in the way that professionals suggest we should. I have all kinds of interesting information stored in my mind, and this is among what's there. I know, for example, that when one goes to relieve oneself, one needs to evacuate quickly, violently, and without strain. If while reading on the toilet you get halfway through *War and Peace* and elimination is still not complete, then it is clear that something is not right and you likely need to adjust your diet so that you can evacuate in a healthy way.

So, at a routine doctor's appointment the doctor asked the parents if they had any questions or concerns. The parents would not say that this was a concern because it was not as bad as I may have suggested, but it was clearly a question the parents had, namely, their daughter was not evacuating effectively, and so what did the doctor suggest? The doctor started by asking if she was eating fruits and vegetables and so on. The parents shared a list of things as best they could, and although they didn't realize that their daughter was listening, she chimed in, "and salad, I also eat a lot of salad"—which she did.

The point of all this is that because she has the freedom to choose what to eat, she has learned to listen to her body and, just as powerful, she has learned about what foods she needs to consume. In fact, on a number of occasions after that she specifically asked her parents for bran cereal because she wasn't feeling quite right. Being a parent, it was endearing to hear about this young child and her ability to understand and appreciate the way her body works in conjunction with the foods she eats.

I am a person of average size, but as a child I was force-fed, and I still find myself compelled to finish everything on my plate, eating way past my level of comfort on far too many occasions. My children almost always leave something on their plates because they are able to pay attention to their internal cues rather than an external order. Often at parties our daughters choose to have very little or nothing at all. Other parents, who are used to force-feeding their children, often question our approach, and some even resort to trying to convince our children that they should be eating. Again, our children are very healthy, active, and have a very good overall self-willed diet.

Similarly, I see parents fretting over whether their children are wearing the right layers of clothing. Again, no one can know how cold or how hot another is. Children are not without sense. They know that if they feel cold they can layer up and if they feel hot they can remove layers. My children will sometimes choose to go outside dressed a certain way and then realize they need to come in and opt for more or less clothing. They can and need to be trusted to make these decisions on their own. Again, they have more than enough sense to do so. Not trusting children to do these things is setting up a situation where they are being deskilled and dumbed-down.

Among the biggest moans, groans, and gripes I hear from young people is their wish that they did not have to go to school. This makes me feel very sad, of course, because, for one, I believe it is unfortunate that they are being institutionalized in places against their will. They are being treated like criminals and are being held against their will and, even worse, their minds, bodies, and spirits are being molded and controlled in ways that many resist. People should be free to be creative, imaginative, and to be encouraged to explore whatever they choose to. Second, learning is a wonderful and beautiful thing, and for so many institutionalized students not to experience and feel the wonder is unconscionable. We should feel ashamed and embarrassed that what we have created results in so many young people being turned off of learning. If we had more trust in ourselves and in them, this would not be the case.

Connected to the subject of this chapter, Holt (1967/1983) writes,

> All I am saying in this book can be summed up in two words—Trust Children. Nothing could be more simple—or more difficult. Difficult, because to trust children we must trust ourselves—and most of us were taught as children that we could not be trusted. And so we go on treating children as we ourselves were treated, calling this "reality," or saying bitterly, "If I could put up with it, they can too." (pp. xii–xiii)

As critical theory reminds us, how we have been conditioned, the discourses that we have internalized, seep through our veins and become powerful memes that we cannot easily shed. It may not be easy, but we can reverse this. As Paulo Freire (1998) points out, "It means that we know ourselves to be *conditioned* but not *determined*" (p. 26). If this is true, and I think it is, then this means that we can overcome our conditioning with hope for a better world as a reward for our progeny and ourselves. If we learn to trust ourselves and realize that we can be trusted to determine what it is we want to learn, for example, then we can more easily trust that others can do the same.

A few years ago my older daughter asked to be signed up for soccer, and we agreed to support her in this endeavour. It was a fairly expensive financial commitment. After a few games, our daughter shared with us that she did not want to continue. She found the beautiful game to be not so beautiful. She felt that it was violent and rough. She is very polite and is not aggressive, so when others would approach the ball she would capitulate and allow them to get it. Coupled with having the adults scream (albeit all with the intent of being supportive), she felt that it was too much. In short, we respected her desire to quit, and she did. At a conference where I was speaking not too long after the incident, I shared my story with the audience and some challenged our wisdom in supporting her decision to quit. They suggested that perhaps we should have forced her to finish her seasonal commitment and then allow her to quit the next season; this way she would not be letting down her team.

They then proceeded to offer another scenario: What if she had the starring role in a play, would we then support her decision to quit? The idea is that she would be letting her team or cast down. Well I thought about this and felt that her decision to not continue was still the right decision. I added to their scenario a scenario of my own. What if, I said, she had broken her leg or worse, what if she could not continue for other medical reasons, would she then be excused? The consensus was unanimous that under those conditions of course she would be excused. So, then, I said, what would happen if her spirit were compromised; would not that be as urgent and legitimate as a broken leg? They agreed that it would.

Children know through reason or intuition when they feel comfortable and when they do not. In fact, they are the only ones that know how it is they feel. They ought to be trusted and listened to. To do otherwise is simply shameful. This is not to say that we cannot ever challenge or offer advice, because of course we can; however, we cannot ultimately impose our will on them if they then decide against us. We need to treat them the way we would treat any other human being: trusting and respecting their own agency. If an adult friend were in the same scenario, how would you act? It is ageist and false to think that children cannot make good decisions in the way that adults can. I know many adults who have made poor decisions, me included, and many children who have made great decisions. Children who know that decisions are theirs to make often consult adults for advice, having learned by experience that these adults have only their interests in mind rather than a manipulative agenda. They trust these adults because the adults have shown they trust the children.

In my own home, I have often been convinced that what I was thinking was the correct way to proceed and what my children were proposing was incorrect, only later to realize that what they were proposing was indeed the correct and sensible path. This is not to suggest that I am a poor parent or that I am a poor adult, but that we all make mistakes and that is just how it is, and some people might suggest that that is how we learn and grow.

We have to trust that life, family, and community are enough to facilitate learning. We need to ensure that young people are in an environment where they feel that they can trust people. They need to feel that they are in a place where they are treated in an honest, fair, and benevolent way. Feeling that you can trust those around you is essential for living a healthy, happy, and peaceful life. The negative impact of being in an environment where trust is lacking is unhealthy, traumatizing, and lasting, whereas, the opposite is nurturing and life affirming. If you are constantly being judged and made to feel that you cannot trust yourself and others, you are constantly living uneasily.

When I was a student, I remember the awful feeling of being in an environment where you feel that you cannot trust yourself, your peers, or the adults. You cannot trust yourself because you are not the ultimate judge of your fate. I remember doing things that I felt relatively proud and confident about, but unfortunately my teachers did not agree with my self-assessment. I had to read things and do things the way they expected things to be done. I had to read and respond in the way that they felt was correct. I could not trust myself and my perspective and my life experience because what I felt and thought did not matter. What the teachers thought was all that mattered. This resulted in things being done as chores and not with love. It meant that I was always afraid, concerned, and ashamed. Always being wrong and even being wrong so often, or not knowing when you are right or wrong, is clearly nerve wracking and damages our psyche and our well-being. It even can impact how you come to view and love yourself.

Looking back with my current perspective, my shame turns to anger and pride. I am angry that others and I were made, and continue to be made, to feel that we were not normal, and I am proud that I did not fit into a system for which I now have so little respect. It is not just the schooling system with which I have issue but also any worldview that is consistent with that philosophy. Whether a teacher or a parent delivers the perspective, the harm is done. Self-directed living mitigates and attempts to eliminate the harm. It is loving and supportive and based in trust.

Trusting peers is also difficult to do in an environment where helping others is considered cheating and everyone is competing for attention, marks, and praise. At some level, if everyone in the classroom is competing, they are all enemies or, at best, rivals. Only one can get the top score. I did not know who to trust, who to confide in, and who would not tell others a secret that I shared so that they could gain praise and I would be condemned. It was difficult to tell when a person would do something hurtful to me so that they would gain acceptance into a community. As a student, I was fairly lucky and was rarely bullied, but the truth is that no one escapes completely unaffected. At one point or another all of us experience moments of rejection. Even those who get into chosen or desired communities are always on edge. They know that getting there does not guarantee that they will be welcomed or allowed to remain. What impact does feeling this lack of trust have? Can we ever recover from this shock? I, for one, still feel the unease from the distrust that has seeped into my being, and I find myself struggling to overcome this unease, as what I know and what I feel battle constantly for supremacy; in other words, my intellect is at war with my emotions.

In our world adults and children are often seen as enemies of each other. It's a struggle: us against them. Adults try to assure young people that what they are being fed is for their own good, like bad-tasting medicine. We create the myth that young people (because of their age alone) cannot understand anything and that they cannot trust themselves simply because they are too young. Young people are being told, and many become convinced, that the information they are being fed is essential. This is perhaps the biggest lie of all. I will continue to say more about this and how it relates to schooling throughout the rest of the book.

Conversely, unschooling, for example, being a willed approach allows for debate, discussion, and dissent. Without this, trust cannot survive. We need to feel that we can dissent, that we can ultimately pave our own paths. Without this freedom, distrust rules. By appealing to a willed approach we are creating respectful environments, which is the subject of the next chapter.

7 RESPECT AND THE WILLED CURRICULUM

In communion with love and trust, respect is equally important. If we are interested in learner-centeredness and democracy, it is critical that we respect people's history, language, and culture and that we respect all beings and the broader world in which we live. Our goal should not be to standardize things, to try to make everyone the same, but to support and understand the value in diversity.

Unfortunately, far too many parents that I speak to share how their children struggled in school because they were considered too active; they could not listen or sit still. Recently, a father shared with me that his daughter has a problem sitting still. I urged that he not use the word problem in that context because a 4-year-old child who does not sit still does not have a problem. Rarely do we ask if it is reasonable to expect children to be so sedentary. Is the problem with the child or with the system that expects "normal" children to be militarily obedient and still? I believe that a society that considers energy, enthusiasm, and eagerness in young people, and all people for that matter, to be problematic is a sick society.

We are so obsessed with our schooling experiment that we are willing to go to great lengths to try to make the system work. So obsessed are we, in fact, that we have resorted even to medicating our children with powerful drugs. It is easier to drug children than to admit that the mainstream schooling experiment is not working or that our worldview needs to change. We have developed such a fundamental faith in schooling that to challenge it is to risk a rebellion. Our goal of increased achievement and improved numbers in the form of test scores is so ingrained that we believe that poisoning children, often with devastating and even fatal effects, is worth the effort.

For example, a report by the International Narcotics Control Board (2010) outlines the following:

> Methylphenidate, amphetamine and dexamphetamine, substances in Schedule II of the 1971 Convention, are used mainly for the treatment of attention deficit disorder (ADD) and narcolepsy. For many years, the most extensive use of those substances for medical purposes has been in the Americas. In recent years, the highest levels of consumption for those stimulants have been observed in Canada, Israel, the United States and countries in northern Europe. (p. 28)

And

> Methylphenidate is the most widely used stimulant in Schedule II of the 1971 Convention. Its manufacture and use continue to increase. In the period 2005-2009, global calculated consumption of methylphenidate increased by 30 per cent, reaching 40 tons, the majority of which was accounted for by the United States. In that country, the use of methylphenidate for the treatment of ADD continues to be promoted in advertisements directed at potential consumers, contrary to the provisions of the 1971 Convention. The use of methylphenidate for the treatment of ADD has been growing in many other countries as well, although the use of the substance continues to be much greater in the United States than in all the other countries combined. Countries other than the United States together accounted for less than 20 per cent of global calculated consumption of methylphenidate in 2000; however, that proportion gradually increased to 30 per cent by 2009. (pp. 28–29)

This is clearly a disrespectful practice, and it is no coincidence that it is attributed to one of the most test-obsessed nations on the planet. Unfortunately, the rest of the world is following along with similar obsessions and a willingness to sacrifice young people's well-being in order to reach arbitrary and artificial goals that many of us believe diminish rather than increase learning and intellectual diversity.

If we truly cared about and respected children and their well-being, their bodies, minds, and spirits, we would not be medicating them the way we do. I do not think that anyone would argue that the children in the USA are so very different from children throughout the world. Given, then, that they are not so different, how can we account for American children being fed such a large percentage of the world's production of methylphenidate?

This lack of respect is not just the domain of adults disrespecting children, but children are also acting disrespectfully towards each other. For example, Craig and Pepler (1998) report that an incidence of bullying happens every 30 minutes in classrooms and every 7 minutes in schoolyards across Ontario. This is a staggeringly large number, when even one incident in a lifetime is too many. Unfortunately, there is no comparison study that I am aware of that looks at unschoolers or other learner-centered democratic approaches like those found in democratic free schools to determine if they fare much better. But what is clear is that people in learner-centered democratic communities are better prepared to deal with this. What I mean is that since the environments encourage respect and self-direction of each individual in real ways, the potential for reducing and dealing with incidents is much greater. For example, within learner-centered democratic spaces and places, anyone can propose rules, challenge rules, write someone up, and have them brought to a judicial committee, as is the case in some free schools and Sudbury Schools. Perhaps most important, these communities see such issues as fundamental and are willing to deal with them in deep, democratic ways, rather than autocratically, often through the use of even more coercion and violence.

Within learner-centered democratic spaces, the message of respect is clear and is taken seriously. In some free schools, for example, students can call a gathering immediately and bring people together to discuss and resolve an issue. The excuse that "we cannot deal with this now because we need to focus on numeracy and literacy to raise test scores" is not an impediment in these environments. As well, within these learner-centered democratic environments, one of the main aims is to facilitate democratic interactions, love, trust, respect, care, and compassion. Achievement scores are not the most important or the primary focus to the exclusion of getting along and respecting others.

Of course lack of respect is not only a mainstream schooling problem. Our society at large also contributes to the lack of respect toward young people. For example, when I see and hear how media celebrates "back-to-school" time as a relief for parents, it makes me feel very uncomfortable. The idea that they promote is that finally getting rid of young people after having them home for the summer is a positive and welcomed event. The message is that parents can now have their time back and that their pesky children will no longer be around to burden them. For me, that this message is so prominent and ubiquitous is shameful and unfortunate. That we have come to imagine our young people as burdens, rather than joys, is something that hopefully we can change. Imagine the outrage that would result if we were to replace the young people in the ads with any other marginalized or not so marginalized group. Thankfully, we can be assured that similar messages against most other beings would not be tolerated, but why does it continue to be acceptable when young people are characterized in that light? Hopefully, you will agree that it should not be tolerated and that we should challenge anyone who delivers this type of unacceptable propaganda. In contrast, a willed curriculum respects all people, beings, and things and is based on love.

In addition, these approaches respect all people's manifestations of personal qualities and abilities. The willed curriculum, for example, is not about forcing people into a standard mold, but it is about valuing everyone's worth as human beings and respecting the decisions that they make. It's not about changing people but about helping them achieve what they choose to achieve. If we respect people enough to allow them to begin with themselves and their personal ambitions and passions, then they will better understand what that means to them and, in turn, they will be able to extend that same respect to others. For me, this is one of the foundations for living democratically and peacefully with each other. If we do not understand, deeply, what respecting the other means, then how can we possibly respect them. We learn about respecting the other by being respected ourselves.

Respecting others is not a process that has an end, but there are lapses, growth, and regressions. It is something that we need to constantly strive toward. I can see that my children have a deep understanding of this and that they really do respond to my challenges of fairness and to my ethical appeals to Kant's categorical imperative. When I ask them how they would feel if the situation were reversed or if they put themselves in my shoes, for example, they quickly and deeply understand. They do so, I believe, because they are living a free life, and so they appreciate their freedom and understand what it means to them, and so in turn they understand deeply what it means to infringe on other people's rights. They would not want it to happen to them, and so they do not do it to others.

Recently (November 2010) I attended a workshop session composed of six teachers and one parent who all shared their experience creating and running mainstream progressive public alternative schools. The people on the panel represented three different alternative public mainstream schools: one was Waldorf inspired, another was focused on social justice and the environment, and the third was holistic based. While they emerged from different concerns, much of what they shared overlapped. All of the schools were very recent start-ups, running for one year or two. They talked about their successes and challenges. They shared inspirational stories about how they imagined different schools and were able to convince the school board to allow them to create these alternative spaces. Their stories highlighted the importance and arbitrariness of having a supportive administration; some schools were lucky enough to have more support than the others. They shared how what the schools are permitted to do is very dependent on who their local administrators are, even though they are a part of the same school board. For example, some are supported and can ignore the grade 3 standardized test that is required by the Ministry in Ontario for all students to write, and some do not have to add letter grades to the reports that go home to parents, and in other cases these allowances are not permitted, depending on who is their administrator. They shared how they were surprised when one school talked about the substantial extra funding they received for teacher development, while the other schools received nothing. They talked about how one small school within a school was able to fundraise $30,000 to buy extra, special, high-quality supplies for their school, such as art supplies. They shared how they all felt that getting young people out into nature was important and how they facilitated this. They shared how they all had to balance the requirements of the local school board and the Ministry's externally imposed curriculum, while staying true to the alternative vision that they created.

Overall, there were ups and downs, and the panel did a great job of sharing what they believed were the ups and of what they believed were the obstacles that they still had to face, largely because of the tension between their vision and school board and Ministry demands that conflicted with their core alternative beliefs. For example, the schools did not approve of standardized testing, grading, and reporting in the way that the Ministry expects. One panelist questioned the motivation behind the board embracing mainstream public alternatives and how things were different in the current context and climate than in the past. She suggested that in the 1970s when mainstream alternatives within the board were created, they were created within a philosophically supportive framework, whereas the context in which they are supported today is based more on economic necessity. The suggestion was that the school board is concerned about declining student enrollment and that creating alternatives is a way of attracting and keeping students that would otherwise choose to go elsewhere.

After listening to each of the schools present for about 20 minutes, we had about an hour for questioning. I asked a question about something I was very curious about but that had not been addressed or hinted at throughout the presentation. In its essence the question was about mutual respect between students on the one hand and teachers and parents on the other. Because I had heard so clearly about how in some cases the presenters felt oppressed by not being supported financially or philosophically to do what they believed they needed to do, I thought that perhaps a group that was living with the struggle to be self-directed and to have their voice heard would be in a good position to empathize and respect the voices of others. I shared with them that I was a child advocate and that I see children as being, unfortunately, the last acceptably oppressed group. The question I asked was the following: Are children's voices being heard and respected within their schools? In other words, if a child resists or chooses to opt out, how do their respective schools deal with this?

Sadly, their responses made me feel very uncomfortable. In sum, they suggested, proudly it seemed, that students did not have a substantive voice and that either the teachers' or parents' voices are what really matter. The parents chose to send the children to these schools, and so the teachers have to remain true to the school's philosophy and ensure that children comply. It is not their job to be oppositional public intellectuals, to use a term from Henri Giroux (2000). I did not follow up, but felt that just hearing them articulate their position was enough. On my way out (I had to leave early), one attendee whispered to me, "Very good question." I wish I could say the same for their responses. Not that they were not clear, thoughtful, and articulate, because they were. What I mean is that I wish that the responses were more supportive and respectful of student voice. I wish that the responses had revealed that of course children's voices are honored in substantive ways, rather than the responses that they gave and of which they were clearly so proud. This is just an example of how far away we are and how much more work needs to be done to better the lives of young people. When even progressives openly accept the victimization of children through oppression and coercion, then we can be assured of how ingrained and entrenched this worldview is.

Does the fact that this view is entrenched and accepted make it right? If we use a deconstructive technique and replace the word "children" in my scenario with any other human group, their response would be overwhelmingly shocking to many more of us. But because we are dealing with young people, and because we see young people in the ways that we do, it seems acceptable for so many (even a progressive group of adults) to advocate for silencing student voices as being the right and sensible thing to do.

Respect needs to be mutual. We need to respect our elders, not simply because they are elder but because we need to respect all humans, beings, and things in our world. After all, younger people, beings, and things are just as deserving of respect as are elders. Imagine how much richer the world would be if respect were not discriminatory, if everyone and everything were understood to be worthy of respect. Unschooling, as a philosophy, demands this. We cannot simply turn respect on and off depending on how old someone is, but it should be at the core of our being.

Within our family, we try to make decisions by reaching a consensus. We earnestly try to meet everyone's needs, though not surprisingly, this is not always possible. However, because we share such strong bonds of mutual respect, when results arise that are unfavorable for one or more of us, there tends to be less of a conflict or fewer hard feelings. For example, if I have a meeting to attend, and my wife is at work, and my parents are busy, and we cannot find alternative arrangements for my daughter, then my daughter may have to concede and come with me, even if she would rather not. Because we as a family try hard to meet everyone's needs, and through experience that usually happens, then the few times that things do not work out are easier to accept. It also makes it easier to concede. I know this happens to me. Because I know how respectful and accommodating they usually are, when the need arises for me to concede, I do so more willingly because I know what they are requesting means a lot to them. It gets to the point where things are done out of love and respect and because a loving and respectful relationship has been established. So, we respect their wishes and they ours, and if occasions arise where this cannot be, they and we understand and appreciate that it is not because of lack of effort but because of forces beyond our control. Contrary to what many may believe, this does not amount to spoiling them. Children cannot be spoiled by being loved, trusted, respected, and treated with care and compassion. Spoiling is an interesting concept. It suggests that we render the child useless for our purposes or make her/his character unfit to be consumed or subsumed by our factory culture. In contrast to the notion of spoiling, I believe that you cannot have too much of these things, as long as everyone understands that it needs to be mutual and that everyone needs to be loved, trusted, respected, and treated with care and compassion.

In the spirit of mutual respect, we try to make decisions together. We try to find solutions together. Our children are included in the decision-making. It's not just something for the adults, but instead we believe that it is for everyone in the community who is involved and impacted to make decisions. As mentioned earlier, if the decision ends up still being unfavorable and we are not creative and imaginative enough to come up with a solution, in the end even an unfavorable decision is easier to stomach because there is faith, respect, and evidence that we tried, and we tried hard, to do things otherwise but simply could not find a solution that works for everyone. It's not up to the adults to come up with a better decision, but it's up to all of us to try to figure out a better solution, and so if we cannot, we cannot, and everyone understands that, because we all genuinely tried. Everyone's voice was listened to and respected, and if at any time someone thinks of another option, then we can always revisit the situation. It's not a competition, a me-against-her, nor is it an us-against-them. We are a team, a family, and we are cooperating with each other in very genuine, organic, and authentic ways. All democratic communities should aspire to work this way.

In sum, as others respect us, we understand what it means to respect ourselves. There are few gifts greater that we can give to each other that compare to the gift of self-respect. The willed curriculum is also all about self-respect. It is about being true to yourself. It is about listening to your inner voice and unfolding and creating yourself. By respecting ourselves we learn to treat others with care and compassion, which is the subject of the next chapter. As we think about caring, we need to be mindful that caring about ourselves too much might foster a sense of selfishness, which could result in the disrespect of others.

8 CARE, COMPASSION, AND THE WILLED CURRICULUM

A few years ago my uncle passed away, and after the funeral we went to my cousin's house to gather and console each other by spending time together. While there, we inevitably started talking about my uncle and the type of man he was and the things he did. As a young person, I loved going to his place, and fortunately he lived close enough to my childhood home for us to visit often. We could easily walk over in about 15 minutes, although we mostly drove. He did not drive and took public transit. He was very gentle and respectful toward me, and we loved to play cards together. He treated me like all adults should treat young people. He did not talk down to me and found ways to include me in the card games. Even when there was an odd number of players, he made sure that we all took turns and had a chance to play, regardless of age. The conversations we had were also very authentic and genuine. It's no wonder I enjoyed going there so much.

As we continued to reminisce after the funeral, my aunt, his wife, shared a story that has remained a very powerful inspiration for me. She shared how one blustery, cold winter day after work my uncle showed up at home without his winter coat on. Naturally, my shocked aunt asked him where his coat was and what he was doing walking around outside on this cold and snowy day without a coat on. It turns out that my uncle had walked past a homeless person who he felt needed a coat much more than he did, and so he had given the man his coat and continued his journey home without one. In thinking about this, I wonder what inspires some of us to participate in acts of care and compassion more often than others among us. Why is it that some people will walk by a needy person and are not moved to act, while others act in very profound ways? Clearly, my uncle did not do this for attention, because none of us knew about this story but my aunt, and the only reason she knew is because she was home when he showed up at the door without his coat. Had she not shared this story with us, we would never have known about it. I often think of this caring and compassionate act and marvel at how inspirational a tale it is for me. His act of kindness and generosity is an example of the potential we all have to be kind and compassionate, to care for others.

But caring decisions are not always simple, and sometimes there are conflicting interests that need to be considered. For example, two people may demand you care at the same time, and you can care for only one of the two. What do we do in these situations? In writing about caring and conflicting decisions, Noddings (1984/2003) says, "It is right or wrong according to how faithfully it was rooted in caring—that is, in a genuine response to the perceived needs of others" (p. 53). She suggests that we cannot decide based on rational decision making whether or not an act is right or wrong, but that there is a turning point. She suggests, "She turns away from the abstract formulation of the problem and looks again at the persons for whom she cares" (p. 53).

At other times the conflict is not between caring for the needs of person A versus person B, but between person A and ourselves. In this situation Noddings (1984/2003) suggests that "I have a picture of those moments in which I was cared for and in which I cared, and I may reach toward this memory and guide my conduct by it if I wish to do so" (p. 80). Later on she clarifies that ethical caring,

> as I have described it, depends not upon rule or principle but

upon the development of an ideal self. It does not depend upon just any ideal of self, but the ideal developed in congruence with one's best remembrance of caring and being cared-for. (p. 94)

This connects well with what I said earlier about modeling and Kant's categorical imperative and how my daughters will know respect by being shown respect, in that the willed curriculum doesn't teach morality, but treats children morally so that they will carry that authentic ethical experience with them and want to share it. She shares how this ethical caring arises out of natural caring, "that relation in which we respond as one-caring out of love and natural inclination" (p. 5).

In writing about "love ethic," bell hooks (2000) writes, "A love ethic presupposes that everyone has the right to be free, to live fully and well" (p. 87). When conflicts arise among families hooks suggests that "healthy families resolve conflict without coercion, shaming, or violence" (p. 211).

As we can see, the practice of being caring and compassionate is simple, yet very difficult. hooks (2000) shares how "we learn compassion by being willing to hear the pain, as well as the joy, of those we love" (p. 165). Once we learn about care and compassion we can then extend our comfort to others. In *Strength to Love*, Martin Luther King Jr (1963/2010) writes, "The hardhearted person lacks the capacity for genuine compassion" (p. 6). Later, of the good Samaritan he writes, "No law in the world could have produced such unalloyed compassion, such genuine love, such thorough altruism" (p. 29). The words of Noddings, hooks, and King should give us a sense of what we need to do and how we need to proceed if we are interested in care and compassion. We need to tap into our natural inclinations and picture moments of when we cared and were cared for, and proceed without coercion, shaming, or violence. We must proceed with compassion and avoid being hardhearted. My uncle's story and many, many more can act as inspiration for each of us. We need to act with these examples at our core. The more stories we share and witness, the more moments we have to picture as we move forward. The question becomes, do we really need MORE stories? Is it quantity over quality? I believe that more just gives us a better chance of finding that one story that really inspires us. Ultimately, we each have to find our own.

Given the importance of these pictured moments in inspiring care and compassion, schools need to be welcoming places where learners, guests, parents, employees, and everyone who walks through the doors are made to feel loved, respected, trusted, and cared for. Everyone needs to feel that they are entering a compassionate environment. Unfortunately, too often this is not the case. For example, whenever I enter my daughter's public school I am made to feel like a criminal, like an unwanted intruder whose presence is treated with suspicion. I am not unjustified in feeling this way but cannot feel otherwise given how others and I are treated whenever we enter the building. Of course, this is not the only school that deals with people in such an uncivil and disrespectful way, but it is the norm and assumed to be arrogantly the correct way to deal with people who enter the building.

I have to say that I rarely enter the building and have done so this school year (2010-2011) only about four times, and even fewer times in the past. Once I was there because my daughter asked me if I would volunteer to accompany her class on a skating trip, once to meet the teacher, once because I was asked to volunteer at a science lesson, and once because my daughter volunteered to bring snacks to class and I helped her carry them in. Unfortunately, each time I felt like an unwanted intruder, and on a few occasions I was treated like one. For example, on one occasion, teachers questioned me as to why I was in the school, and I was corralled to the office and asked to wait there because my daughters and I could not be wandering the halls unaccompanied. The worst part of all is that the way I was treated is lauded and assumed to be good practice by many.

As mentioned earlier, I am not the only one who is treated this way, nor is this the only school with these policies in place. Another parent shared with me how a guest principal physically blockaded the front door and maneuvered to prevent her from entering the school. The principal told the parent that she could not enter the premises. For the most part, parents are not allowed to enter the school, nor are the children, outside of specified times that are dictated by the guardians of the school. Surely, there are better ways. Surely, we can do better than creating an atmosphere of fear, discomfort, and nonacceptance. Surely, we can create spaces and places that do not assume that everyone who enters is a criminal and has no right to be there. Surely, we can create spaces and places where the default is not characterized by an unwelcoming environment that is suspicious of everyone, and create instead one that is more welcoming and embracing. When schools treat parents and visitors this way, what they are doing is modeling to the young people a very undemocratic and unwelcoming way that people deal with other people.

In fact, the school seems to try hard to keep parents out. On the first day of school, the students, often accompanied by the parents, line up outside and the teachers come out to meet them, rather than having the parents enter the school with the children so that they can all embrace and meet in a loving, communal gathering. I do not know if the reason for this is explicitly to keep parents out, but the results are ultimately the same.

Furthermore, the school is so aggressive that they have sent out letters warning parents about procedures they need to follow when dropping off their children, and in the letter they threatened to have a vehicle ticketing officer enforce the threats, and they did and do follow through with this. Clearly, the problem is not parents dropping off their children, but the problem is the lack of space and infrastructure to support this necessity. Again, the result is an unwelcoming environment where parents are made to feel unwanted, where they are threatened, punished, and bullied. But this is not what is the most reprehensible part in all of this; the most reprehensible part is that this is seen to be commonsensical. They do not see the solutions they have come up with as a problem, but they see their solutions as the correct and appropriate response. I see this as an arrogant and limited vision of what could and should be possible. Schools could be treated as an extension of family; a school could be a community hub, a place where people are welcomed and relationships are built, rather than being isolated and isolating restricted zones. If school leaders are not creative and imaginative enough to create welcoming spaces and places, then we should replace their narrow visions with more hopeful and communal visions. To criminalize everyone and treat everyone as suspicious is not the way to create community. So, it seems clear to me that love, trust, respect, care, and compassion are not what the aim of mainstream schooling is, but it seems like its aims are to create isolated factories where children work as if they are in sweatshops to prepare to serve and not ask questions.

We need to stop mistreating children in schools. We have ignored for far too long that children are people with feelings. We cannot continue to damage their bodies, minds, and spirits. Young children are not unfeeling objects that we can mold, manipulate, and contort. In fact, such treatment will eventually lead children to the breaking point. Yet, far too many of us treat children in such way. As an example, recently a young friend of mine and I were having a conversation and she shared some profound injustices that were done to her, ones that happen daily in schools but which are atrocious. I have to preface that this 7-year-old is bright, articulate, and has untold gifts. She is a joy. What is being done to her and countless other children all over the world is something that we should all take blame for and for which we should all be ashamed. When I share with you what I find to be so atrocious, many will see it as just part of everyday life; I hope to reframe this and argue that these everyday practices are wounding our children and harming our world. They are not moving to create a caring and compassionate world, but instead an uncaring and uncompassionate one.

First, I want to make my stand on grading clear once again. I believe that grading is a dehumanizing, limiting activity and a way of manipulating many people to do things that they would otherwise choose not to do. Having said that, this young girl is a straight "A" student. Again those who get "As" are just as damaged by the grading system as those that get lower grades. So, this girl shared that she received a B- on a math test. This fact was eating away at her very core. When we judge people this way, this judgment is not neutral, but biting. It is a blow to a person's well-being. It destroys people's self-images and destroys their self-worth. People are not unfeeling objects that we can pound away at without destroying their inner selves. Again, this is made more shameful when we consider how students feel that what we are teaching, assessing, and evaluating them on, in so many cases, is arbitrary, narrow, and disconnected from their interests and passions.

Second, this young girl, who has received great praise for her piano playing and recitals in the past, was very excited about sharing her gifts with her school community by playing at the local talent show. Unfortunately, once again the decision went against her. She was denied entrance to the talent show. She was cut and did not make it. The young girl's mom shared with me that she approached the lead teacher one day after school in the playground and the teacher said simply that she agreed that all children should have a chance to perform and to shine, but that the teachers did not want to take two nights out of their week to supervise the talent show and so they had to limit the number of children that were accepted. Clearly, there are other solutions. Personally, I believe that the cost of supervising another night pales in comparison to destroying someone's self-worth. And again, there are clearly other solutions. They could ask for parent volunteers so each teacher would have to supervise for only one night. They can limit the performance time each child has, or they could break down the performance into smaller groups so that everyone can participate, and so on. The point of these activities is to get young people to feel loved and valued, not to have them feel destroyed. I have been to talent shows within the unschooling community, where all those who choose to share their talent are given a forum and where no one is excluded. I strongly believe that this is how it should be. This is how communities are built, and this is how people are respected. Those who go to an amateur talent show, I think, understand that this is simply a celebration and an exercise in community building and spirit building. The competitive nature of many mainstream schooling talent shows simply ignores people's feelings. It ignores what is the essence of care and compassion. It provides awful examples for us to picture when we consider what it means to be caring and compassionate

On a similar note, another mother shared with me that her daughter and her friends spent the whole school year rehearsing and preparing for their school talent show. They purchased uniforms and were really, really excited about participating. Unfortunately, they too were devastated by not making the final cut. Again, these are feeling human young people that we are dealing with, and we need to deal with them in much more humane ways. We cannot simply and continually squash their enthusiasm without doing considerable damage. Clearly, I am not condoning violence against schools, but given this slow and steady, and sometimes not so slow, abuse that schooling inflicts on its charges, is it really that surprising that unfortunately so many go back and exact vengeance on the schools they attended? Imagine how wounded people have to feel and how broken they have to be to resort to such atrocious acts. Kirsten Olson's (2009) book titled *Wounded by School: Recapturing the Joy in Learning and Standing Up to Old School Culture* comes to mind here. This is not to deny that there are also people who go back to their former schools and give them accolades and praises for the experiences they had there. But how many of these have actually taken the time to consider how their overall schooling experience has wounded them? In my experience in talking with people and teaching adult learners, I find that many do not think about schooling as being something that has wounded them. In part, this is all about Freire's (1970/2000) conscientization where he argues that without awareness, the oppressed exist in a reality which frustrates their interests. It is a struggle where they are "at one and the same time themselves and the oppressor whose consciousness they have internalized" (p. 48).

However, when we do begin to think about how damaging their overall experience was, then even those who have thought of themselves as being "successful" students begin to process their experience as damaging when they see schooling through an unschooling worldview, one that focuses on love, trust, respect, caring, and compassion

The third thing that this young, athletic 7-year-old shared with me was her experience trying out for the track team. Again, she was excited and revved up for the tryouts. Unfortunately, once again she did not make it. They accepted five people and she came in sixth. As I said before, when we do this to young people we are inflicting a serious and negative impact on their self-worth and on what it means to be caring and compassionate. It is as if mainstream schooling has more respect for rules than for children. These are feeling humans whose bodies, minds, and spirits are constantly being chipped away. A feeling adult world would not allow this abuse to happen, and the fact that we do speaks volumes about how troubled we are and how urgent it is for us to heal. Joining track should be about fun and physical fitness, not about destroying spirit. Standage et al. (2003) found that an overreliance on game play in which success is viewed in terms of winning or losing can have a negative effect on student engagement in physical education (as paraphrased in Bevans, Fitzpatrick, Sanchez, & Forrest, 2010).

In my experience, young people love to play games without keeping score, to play just for the fun of it. Many of my young friends and loved ones have taught me the joy of this, and I have come to embrace how great this noncompetitive way of playing is. For example, even playing Scrabble can be loads of fun without keeping score, and the same goes for any other game. I wish that game developers would create games where keeping score, losing, and other competitive functions could be disabled.

Some argue that competition presents lessons that prepare children for winning and losing in the adult world. Perhaps if we were more sensitive and caring to our young people, our adult world would better reflect sensitivity and caring toward ourselves, others, and the world. I think this argument is best challenged by Presnitz (2011), who reminds us of what Holt once said: "That line of thinking means that since adults experience a lot of headaches, we should put our children's heads in vices each day so they can prepare for what it feels like to be an adult" (p. 20).

Young people are being harmed and wounded, and by extension so is our society, because of schooling and its prevailing worldview. If young people were not in school, or at least not in schools that create these harmful competitive battles, then they would be exposed to more modeling of what it means to act in a loving way. Having children constantly compete and compare how well they are doing against others and against narrow measures results in their internalizing the wrong messages, and their self-confidence and self-worth are constantly being battered. For example, with respect to literacy, if young people did not know what level they are reading at in comparison to others who may be measuring above or below them, then they would feel successful at the stage they are at, as they should. In other words, if we take reading as an example, then the level they are reading at is the level they should be reading at, because we all learn to read at different times, and the overwhelming majority of us will learn to read painlessly if we are allowed to do so naturally and when we are ready, so it does not make sense to forcefully push people in directions that they are resisting. Having people learn to read in natural and gentle ways is a positive thing and not something negative. Some learn slower and some faster, so where they are is where they should be. It is not a race, and having those learning to read slow down, work at their own pace, and within their own interests results in confidence building. One of my former students shares a Nigerian saying that is appropriate here: "Wherever you can get to by running, you can get to by walking." The flaneur knows that walking allows us to stroll, see, hear, touch, and observe, whereas running or driving by quickly results in an experience where much is missed. After all, if the goal is to enjoy the journey, more specifically to enjoy reading, then we need to create noncompetitive and joyful experiences around reading, rather than anxiety, pressure, and fear.

Ranking is also contrary to the principles of care and compassion. Being told that you are below average is clearly not a good thing, and being told that you are above average creates tension and pressure to maintain that status, and no one wants to be just average, so why rank people? We notice that people are good at and interested in different things, and this diversity should be celebrated. As well, when we consider out-of-school factors, we need to understand that those who have a harder and less privileged upbringing need more love and supportive environments and not undemocratic competitive spaces like the ones that result from mainstream schooling.

Recently, I attended a series of presentations delivered by employees of the Ontario Ministry of Education. While listening to the presentations I was struck by how similar-sounding the words used by unschoolers are to those used by mainstream schoolers. For example, mainstream schoolers talk about differentiated instruction, differentiated curriculum, authentic learning, being student centered, the importance of play, and so on. Given the similarity between some mainstream schooling terms and the language used by unschoolers, why is there such a difference in practice? It seems to me that one large difference is that given the rules and regulations and obstacles faced by mainstream schoolers, they cannot take these concepts seriously in their practice, whereas those who are interested in the willed curriculum can actually take these philosophical starting points seriously. In other words, these concepts cannot work given how mainstream schooling is set up, even though those in mainstream schooling clearly feel that these concepts are important. That they feel that these terms are wothwhile is evidenced by how often they speak and write these terms in their presentations and documents. Unfortunately, for mainstream schooling these laudable concepts that scream care and compassion remain only concepts and are not practiced, and fortunately for those who practice a willed curriculum these concepts are real and are often realized. Those who practice the willed curriculum can differentiate instruction given the needs and wants of the learner, they can differentiate the curriculum for each and every learner, they can make the learning experienced authentic by connecting with the world or by listening to the learner and taking what the learner needs seriously, and of course they can place the learner at the center, allowing her/him to learn what, when, where, how, and why she wants. Furthermore, by doing and taking these concepts seriously and implementing them in practice, we are practicing care and compassion.

Furthermore, I know that when mainstream schoolers talk about differentiated instruction, differentiated curriculum, authentic learning, being student centered, and the importance of play, they do not mean what I mean by these terms. I know this because of the answers I received to the questions I posed to them in trying to clarify what and how they understand these concepts. Their answers were far from consistent with learner-centered democratic practices, and learner voice, and agency; instead, their responses placed the curriculum and Ministry mandates at the center. Ultimately, as one of my graduate students once asked me, if I have to plan so far in advance, and have my long-range plans ready before I even meet my students, then how can what we are expected to do truly be learner centered? Similarly, it was clear to me from the responses I received to my probing that ultimately it is not the students at the center, it is the curriculum. This is evident also by looking at the tools and technology that are used to ensure that teachers comply with the mandated curriculum. I am thinking here, for example, of report cards. Report cards are not merely a neutral tool but a technology that is used to ensure that what those in positions of power deem to be important is being "covered" by the teachers and "learned" by the students. Report cards are tools that limit and control what people can do, and given the increasing level of detail on what teachers need to report on and how often, it is clear that the control is becoming more intrusive. For example, in Ontario in the elementary math portion of the report card, it is no longer simply an overall math grade that teachers have to report on, but they have to report a grade for specific strands. This level of detail means that report cards are tools used to ensure that teachers are complying, and the result is a curriculum-centered, rather than a learner-centered, environment. Again, this is very inconsistent with a system that takes care and compassion seriously. So, instead we need one that makes learners feel loved, respected, trusted, and cared for rather than one that ignores the individual and the community in favor of an externally imposed curriculum. An environment that places the desires of those in positions of power before the needs and wants of learners is far from a caring and compassionate one. So what is the willed curriculum anyway? The next chapter will continue to focus on revealing this.

9 THE WILLED CURRICULUM

Among the various curricula documented and written about are the recommended curriculum, the written curriculum, the taught curriculum, the supported curriculum, the assessed curriculum, the learned curriculum, and the hidden curriculum. Each of these curriculum labels focuses on a different issue affecting children and schools. The one that I am most interested in discussing is one I have called the willed curriculum. One of the most powerful features of the willed curriculum is that it is emergent and not rigidly preplanned. Throughout this chapter I will provide specific examples of how the willed curriculum has evolved throughout our family's lived unschooling experience. A few questions that are always foremost on many new and practicing unschoolers' minds are the following: How do I unschool? Am I doing unschooling right? After reading this chapter you will have a good sense of how organic, emergent, and exciting the willed curriculum is, and you can begin to include it within your own context, whether in your home, school, place of work, or any other context you are in.

 The reason I call it the willed curriculum is because it is inspired and driven by the will of the learner. The willed curriculum is what drives many hobbyists and amateurs to create and invest in things that arise from their will, from their own desire. I propose that the willed curriculum is the most exciting of all the various categorizations of curriculum because it is driven by the learner's internal motivation and will to explore. For example, I recall, when my younger daughter was 5, how she was engaged in a workbook. She was working on a page with many images, and for whatever reason the image of a yak caught her attention. I asked her if she would like to Google it and then use Google Image to see pictures of yaks, and she said that she would. So she clicked Safari on our Mac, and in Google typed in the word yak; she then clicked Images. She noticed that some of the images were coloring sheets. She asked if she could print and color them. I mentioned that of course she could. I told her that I needed to do work on the laptop and suggested she go into the den and turn on the Windows-based desktop and use that to print the coloring pages she desired. She then came back to me and asked if, instead of printing the coloring sheets, she could actually print the images of some of the yaks. Again, I said that of course she could. Her interests grew from printing yaks to printing other animals that caught her interest. After each image was printed she cut it out using scissors. When she finished printing a number of images she came to me and asked me what a particular image she had was. I mentioned to her that I thought it was a bison. I went with her into the den, and sure enough, it was an American Bison. At that point, I suggested that she write down the names of each of the animals on the back of the printed cutout sheets so that we know what they are. She mentioned that that was her plan all along and that she was planning to go back and do that once she finished printing what she wanted to print. I suggested that it might be easier if she just wrote the names as she went along so she did not have to backtrack. She agreed and so backtracked to write the names of the ones she had printed so far and from then on started writing the names as she went along.

 I want to mention that while I was in my room doing work, I was able to make out some of the things she was talking to herself out loud about while engaging in her willed curriculum. One statement that sticks out in my mind was that she excitedly exclaimed, "I can't believe I am so interested in yaks." Ultimately, she decided that she would make a book out of her printed images, and so she proceeded to place them in order and to staple the pages together. She then shared her book with her sister and mom. She started the project at around 9 in the morning and it was complete by around 6 p.m. Throughout that time she took time off to eat and spent about 3 hours playing with friends. For most of the rest of the time she was engaged in creating what ultimately became a book.

On another occasion, when she was 6, I shared with her that the largest newspaper in Canada by circulation numbers is running a series whereby they ask readers to submit images of wildlife that they see around their community. In short, this captured my daughter's interest. She thought that this was great and that it was something that she would like to do. She retrieved our camera and went around our house and took pictures of worms, bugs, caterpillars, ants, and so on. She said she did not want to take images of birds because the series had quite a few birds and she felt that that would reduce the likelihood that they would accept another bird. She was having so much fun that she infected me with her enthusiasm, and when she asked if I would like to join her I enthusiastically agreed. Together we continued to snap photos. When we thought we had some good shots we proceeded to download the images onto the computer. We decided that a shot of an ant with something in its mouth (that we shot on our front lawn where there is an anthill) would be the image we would go with. We cropped the image, saved it, and she went into her email and submitted it to the paper. She was excited all day. She kept checking her email in case the editors emailed her back. The next day, I woke up at my usual time, long before the girls got up, and to my pleasure the image was posted online with the caption, "Hard-working ant. Karina Ricci Photo. 6-year-old Karina Ricci sends us a photo of a hard-working ant carrying something in its mouth." When we shared the great news with her, she shared how she had hoped all night that the picture would be published. Every day my girls surprise me with imaginative and creative things that they decide to do. They are

THE WILLED CURRICULUM, UNSCHOOLING, AND SELF-DIRECTION

always engaged in doing something, and clearly what they decide to do on their own is not something that I, or anyone else, can improve on. The learning that happens as they engage in these activities is meaningful to them, deep, authentic, and very, very rich.

The willed curriculum is not an unusual event but is something that we experience on a daily basis. It is not a deviation from many everyday routines but, in fact, it is a process that happens many, many times a day, day in and day out, to all of us. It is not something unusual or strange, but if we pay attention to how we live our lives we will quickly realize that we are making use of the willed curriculum already, and often with powerful and dramatic learning results. In this sense, the willed curriculum is not a call for something new but a call to be more mindful and make more use of something we are already using. We know that interest and internal motivation are critical for deep learning. Loving what we are learning, interest, and internal motivation are at the very core of the willed curriculum.

For example, in the yak activity outlined above, the learning that happened while she was engaged is tremendous and far more nuanced than anything I could have preplanned. While following her interest at that time, she learned about different animals, she cut, she wrote, she counted, she manipulated a computer (both a Mac and a Windows-based computer), she printed, she stapled, and she did it all from a place of love. She was not forced or manipulated. She was not assigned tasks or tested. She simply followed her interests. She used her imagination and creativity to create her book, which, I believe, resulted in a richer learning experience than anything I could have planned for her. I believe that if I had insisted that she needed to work in her workbook, and this was workbook time, and that she could use the computer once she was done with the exercises in her workbook, I would have likely ruined a great day. In addition, I would have sent her the message that what she chooses to do, that listening to her inner voice, is not as important as following someone else's idea of what matters and of what she should be doing. I want to make clear again that even the decision to work in her workbook was hers, not mine. In fact, the workbook she was working on was one that I printed off the Internet from a site that has worksheets in various subjects sorted by grades because she asked me if I could find and print some off for her. So, I printed what amounted to 200-plus pages and hole-punched and placed them in a binder for her, so that whenever she wills it, she can do with it as she pleases. In fact, she completed the binder at her own pace and in her own time. This was her third workbook that deals with curriculum for 5- and 6-year-olds that she has completed since September 2010, and as I write this we are in November 2010. So, she has completed about 600 to 700 pages of worksheets, among the other things that she does. Admittedly, I am not a fan of these resources, but it is her decision, as I have argued throughout. This is another reason why it is so important to allow the learner to take control; otherwise our biases will limit what they do. It seems almost overwhelming for a 5-year-old to do so much, but the truth is that she completed one workbook in about 2 mornings and then asked for more. She has a very balanced and fun life. She reads books, sings, dances, loves to use our camera to take pictures of things she has completed, she paints, uses play dough, cooks, does chores, swims, skates, rides a two-wheeler, plays hockey, plays constantly with friends, plays the piano, the recorder, and the guitar, does crafts, relaxes, and on and on. She does not do these things on my schedule, but she simply follows her will. She is very focused and can spend hours and hours doing things. She has tremendous energy and is in great shape. Starting in September 2010, she spends three afternoons a week in various classes that she enjoys: a cooking class, a science class, and an art class. She is free to opt out anytime she chooses, and she is well aware of that. I cannot fully describe how rich and varied her life is, because she is constantly doing things that make documenting and evaluating it all impossible, and in a sense pointless, because each of us has to create our own path and not follow someone else's, and we will follow our own path if given the freedom to do so.

She constantly amazes me with the curriculum that she creates for herself. Both of my daughters do. For example, when my older daughter was 7 years old, she decided to craft a dog. When she told me, I said that would be a fine idea. She made a beautiful face of a dog and showed it to me. It was cut out and cute. I then simply suggested that it would be neat to make a body and paste the head onto it. She thought that that was a great idea and said that she was planning to do that next. After she made the body she showed it to her younger sister, who then suggested that she should make a collar and leash out of plumbing pipe. Again, she thought that it was a great idea, and so she proceeded to do that. Then, she suggested that she would like to make fur for it. I suggested that it would be really, really cool if she glued cotton balls and made that the fur. She again agreed, and she went off to add cotton balls. She added them to both sides. Finally, I suggested booties, and the project was complete. It is one of the ones that she is most proud of. The dog was then named Fluffy and was a regular part of the girls' imaginative play for awhile. The project was willed by her and was emergent. Others made suggestions and she was free to accept or reject what was said to her.

The girls make use of contemporary tools to help them learn what they are interested in learning about. Unfortunately, in many schools and school boards many powerful contemporary and preeminent tools of learning and websites are banned. They are considered distractions and a waste of time. The more I witness how my daughters and others make use of these tools, the more idiotic the bans appear. Recently (when she was 7 years old), Annabel wanted to learn to play the recorder, and so she used YouTube to find someone offering lessons and she then proceeded to follow along with the lessons. These were prerecorded videos that were replayed on YouTube, but for those who are interested there are real-time people offering real-time lessons remotely, some for a fee and some for free. They use Skype or some other service that allows them to video link with each other and communicate in real time. These tools are increasing and are making the willed curriculum easier to practice. If there is not someone within your local community that shares your interest or the expertise you need, you can always use technology to log into the global community and connect with someone in that way.

Technology is also making it easier to find like-minded people and communities both online and within our local neighborhoods. There are many list-serve groups that act as initial points of contact for those searching for like-minded people, whereby people hook up online and then arrange events or arrange to gather at certain locations. Perhaps, the increase in interest in unschooling and homeschooling, in general, is a direct result of technology and its ability to disseminate information and create community.

It is wonderful to watch how my daughters continue to grow and learn to be self-sufficient. One day, when Karina was 5, my mom came over and Karina wanted French fries. My mom said that she would love to help her with that but that she did not know how to work our oven. Karina, to my mom's surprise, proceeded to make her own fries, which included turning our oven on.

People learn to use life tools in very seamless ways if given a chance. For example, when the girls were 5 and 7, there was a film crew over at our place. They were there to interview me and to take some footage of my family. After they put their camera away and were all packed up, Karina decided that she wanted to call her friend. They were surprised when Karina picked up the phone and dialed her friend's number. We were not surprised, since she has been doing this for a while and she has quite a few numbers memorized. My hope is that we can get to a stage where a 5-year-old dialing a phone to call someone is not shocking to adults. If they are given the chance and the freedom, trust, and respect, we will quickly realize how capable young people are. If we look at other cultures and search throughout history we can see how capable young people are and have been. I am not suggesting that we recreate what, in some cases, were oppressive and exploitative conditions for young people simply because they are capable, but what I am suggesting is that we shed our erroneous beliefs about young people and their feebleness, whether it be physical, intellectual, moral, emotional, or spiritual.

Also by spending time in the world with us, they learn a lot about the world. For example, our girls run errands with us, use the bank machine, have attended funeral homes, and been to dealerships, grocery shopping, they have come to work with us, attended conferences, traveled with us, and so on. I believe that spending time with us, as we live our lives, both enriches our relationships and helps them better understand how the world works. In short, they participate in the adult world and by doing so learn about what it means to be an adult. This is why we often discuss finances with them and other adult burdens and pleasures so that they know how the world works.

Theirs is a truly holistic curriculum of and for life. When things go wrong, for example, we do not shoo them away, but we gather them around. We do not ask them to leave the tools alone, but to pick them up and help in any way they will. It's not an adult effort, but a family effort. When the shower drain recently clogged, they were there, ready, willing, and eager to help. Same with when the fireplace was not working properly, and when some walls needed to be touched up and repainted. Their holistic curriculum of life means that they are in charge of their own hygiene and have been since they were very, very little. They participate in the adult world, attend concerts, go to the zoo, museums, farms, banks, doctors' offices, car repair shops, malls, charities, and so on. When we cannot handle the job and need the assistance of repair people, they are there to watch, and they love to watch. You could not pry them away. Recently, my daughter and I were off to see the new Harry Potter film, something that she was eagerly anticipating. Just before we left we received a call that one of our friendly repairpersons was coming over. My daughter asked if we could wait until he arrived so she could be a part of the event. Fortunately, he left on time and we made it to the screening of Harry Potter at our scheduled time. I share this because, to me, it is an indication of how eager younger people are to be a part of the adult world. They help garden and rake leaves, they do chores, and they do these things willingly, albeit sometimes leaving before the task is done, sometimes returning, and sometimes not. But they are always ready to give it a go again the next time. In fact, today (15 June 2011) I mentioned that I am going to wash the windows in our home, both outside and inside. Annabel was so upset at the possibility of missing out on helping out with this that she had me promise that I would wait until after school to do this so that she can help out as well. Many believe that children do not like or want to do chores, but for many the truth may be very different, when, for example, children know their help is truly wanted.

As well, as my children try to learn about the world no subject is taboo. They have requested and have watched live births on the Internet, they skim the newspapers, and watch the news daily. They know that there are those who work towards war and destruction and that there are those who work towards peace, and that sometimes the warriors are thought of as peacekeepers. There is no better preparation for living life than to live life, to understand life in ways that adults do. And this phrase is not mere tautology, for "prepare" means to make ready in advance. It seems to me that the only aspects of life we can hope to make ourselves somewhat ready for would be those things with which we have already had some experience. So, living life does make us ready for life. Keeping children from real-life experience simply delays their life and cheats them out of the chance to have real preparation to unfold as they live. By preparing them solely with the experience and to follow the directives of others, adults cheat them out of the chance to unfold as individuals through their own discovery. This is not to suggest that adults have all of the answers. In fact, we do not have all of the answers, and when we do not, it is important that they know that we do not, or that people disagree on this or that issue, and so there are differing views. Many parenting "experts" urge parents to have a united front regardless of whether they are right, so that the children do not see them disagree. I think this is a shame, and it also deprives young people from witnessing a healthy reality. People disagree, and solutions need to be had and compromises reached. This needs to be modeled and witnessed.

It is endearing to watch Karina flip through the newspaper, looking for pictures that catch her eye. Sometimes, as I read the newspaper, the girls cuddle beside me or look over my shoulder, and they ask questions about whatever catches their interest. The world is a wonderful, awful place, and when they are ready for that truth they will ask about it, and we will do our best to try to make sense of it together. A holistic curriculum for life is not a closed, hidden secret but an open, embracing part of their reality. Again, there is no greater preparation for life than to live life.

Much of what happens in schools is not preparation for life but merely busy work that is disconnected and that does not resonate with people. For example, I have often wondered what would happen if some of my colleagues and I, or "successful" (whatever that means) adults in general, would write the final exams along with grade 9 students. I suspect that many of us would fail miserably in many areas. This is not a reflection on us but a reflection on how little connection there is between the school curriculum and life. We have to remember that math that is taught in school is usually not the type of math that most people will have to deal with as they live their lives; most of that school math, most of us will likely never use. Again, if given a chance, learners will create a more rigorous and meaningful curriculum for themselves than anyone external to their being can ever create.

I have found that when young people see things in the world, they often make that event a part of their play. Free play I believe is extremely important to learning. For example, after attending a cruise, our children played an elaborate cruise ship game where they turned our home into cabins and so on. They did the same after we attended a wedding, they created a wedding-themed game; after being on an airplane, they played an airplane game; after going to the doctor, they played a doctor game; after going to the dentist, they played a dentist game; after we went to our cousin's new condo, they transformed our house into an apartment. The same happened after going to the bank, grocery shopping, traveling, movie theatre, sporting event, restaurant, circus, horseback riding, the zoo, hairdresser, and so on. Play is a way for them to internalize and embody what it means to be a part of the world in various roles or ways.

One of the games they like playing most is school. It is very enlightening to witness this game in action and how they recreate the oppressive conditions as they play. For example, during play they replicate how students need to be silent and can speak only when the teacher gives the student permission. The student is often forced to sit with legs crossed and still. They take attendance, assign homework, give tests, and so on. It is powerful to witness how engrained and entrenched the roles and the culture and practices of schooling are as they play. It is fascinating to watch as they act out the roles, both perceived and experienced in the world and through other cultural and constructed representations of schooling in various mediums such as television.

For many things, ultimately, there is no substitute for real-world experiences. Reading it in a book or watching it on television or the Internet does not leave the same impressions as experiencing it in reallife situations. So, for example, reading about being in a condominium, or watching characters on television living or interacting in a condominium is not the same as actually spending time walking through, exploring, and experiencing condominium living. The same with schools; learning about things secondhand is nowhere near the experience of living things firsthand where the positives and negatives become a part of our embodied, holistic, lived experiences. To truly understand, appreciate, and connect with the world, we need to live within it, move around it, and explore it. As so often happens in schools, there is no need to predetermine what they are going to learn from the experience before they experience it, but instead they should simply experience it. After experiencing it, they can then talk about it, play about it, think about it, dream about it, imagine about it, and create and recreate it in any way they like. Ultimately, whether they act it out, write about it, draw it out, or, if they choose, do nothing and move on to the next experience, the decision needs to be theirs.

Karina tying her shoes

The best time to learn things is when they are ready and motivated to learn something. Deep learning happens when they are interested in learning something, and not because someone believes that they should know something. For example, in the past, I offered to show Karina how to tie her shoes and she always politely declined, until yesterday (15 February 2011). You see, up until now she had no reason to learn how to tie her shoes, because she did not own shoes with laces. The shoes she preferred were ones without laces. However, yesterday she and her mom went out to buy a new pair of shoes, and the shoes she chose have laces. So, as soon as she came home, she proudly showed me her new shoes and asked me if I could show her how to tie them. Of course, I agreed. The whole thing took a matter of minutes. I do not mean 10 or 15 minutes, but literally minutes, or perhaps it's more accurate to say seconds. I am sure that I could have forced her to learn to tie her shoes sooner, perhaps years sooner. I would imagine that the process would have been painful and frustrating for both of us and not the pleasant and enjoyable celebration that it turned out to be. This is what is sometimes powerfully characterized as the difference between just-in-time learning as opposed to just-in-case learning. Just-in-case learning is where you learn something just in case you will need to use it sometime in the future, whereas just-in-time learning is learning that happens when it is needed and therefore is a more relevant, deep, and meaningful type of learning. Often, the result is that if you learn it and don't need it, you forget what you learned and have to relearn it anyway. So how did she learn to tie her shoes?

The story of how she learned to tie her shoes is as follows: We both sat on my bed and made ourselves very comfortable. I was sitting up behind her and she was sitting up in between my legs. I asked her which shoe she wanted to tie first, the right or the left. She chose the left, so I took the right. We placed the shoes in front of us without her feet in them. I showed her once: cross the laces, make bunny ears (I still tie my shoes this way), cross the bunny ears, loop one underneath, pull, and that's it. She had two problems that she asked me to help her solve. So I suggested that after she makes the bunny ears she needs to cross them higher, and when she pulls the laces, to pull from the string not directly linked to the aglet, because if she pulls the area immediately connected to the aglet, it will come undone.

Just like when I showed Annabel how to tie her shoes, I found that she wanted to practice on her own without my directing or commenting on her every move. I assured her that with practice things would get easier and that the final tie would be tighter. The next day, she tried and was frustrated because she was unable to do it. I showed her again, but this time she was not in the right frame to tackle the task. I suggested she just leave it for now and try again later. She did. About 30 minutes later she came upstairs where I was with both shoes perfectly tied and as happy as can be. She has not looked back since. I believe that the key was that she learned to tie her shoes not because sometime in the future she would have to tie them, but because she had shoes that needed tying. I believe that the same could be applied to learning matrix algebra if she decided she wanted to try her hand at computer programming—simple or complex, it would still be just-in-time. Years of math drills and exercises cannot take the place of authentic experiences in analytical thinking. Even with other children, I've noticed that the intermediate skills needed to complete some task they are interested in are often learned rapidly and efficiently. Outside the context of an inspiring project, mastering those skills would be drudgery as Thomas Moore suggests: To be educated, a person doesn't have to know much or be informed, but he or she does have to have been exposed vulnerably to the transformative events of an engaged life. This same basic principle of deep, organic, natural, and authentic learning applies to the willed curriculum, which encourages this, as do unschooling and other learner-centered democratic approaches. It encourages a type of learning that is much more authentic, real, organic, and gentler than the learning that so often happens in schools. I will say more about the difference between schooling and unschooling, which is the subject of the next chapter.

But before I do, it is crucial to note that although my daughters' lives are rich in the ways I have outlined, including easy access to multiple computers and other technological resources, I do not want to suggest that this is a requirement for learning about the world and finding your place in it because, in contrast, my upbringing was not rich in these ways, although it was rich in love. My point is that there is not one path but many diverse and contradictory paths that people take as they live life. My family is merely one example, and there are as many examples as there are families.

10 THE WILLED CURRICULUM: SOULFUL SPACES

When I think of soulful spaces I think of spaces that are respectful and that allow the people the time they need to unfold and create themselves. In this chapter I will share why I believe that mainstream schools are not soulful spaces and share some examples of alternative schools and educational possibilities that I believe are. I will argue that we need to make the shift to these more soulful spaces because it is the ethical thing to do. The focus will also be on how, by allowing children the space to form themselves, the world will be transformed. If we want a better future, we need to start by rethinking our child-rearing practices. We cannot expect people to be treated a certain way for so many years and for them to suddenly forget the wounds that they have received as young people. Although we are conditioned and not determined, we often act in ways that are consistent with our conditioning, so if we were wounded as children we are more likely to wound as adults. Memes are just as difficult to overcome as genetic predispositions. In other words, as adults we often act in ways that have been modeled for us when we were younger. Since a healthy, strong community is based on the health and strength of its individuals, which begins with our child-rearing practices, we need to be sure that our child-rearing practices are consistent with the world we desire. After all, the willed curriculum is about how to improve learning. It is about how we learn best.

Defining Soulful Spaces

I am using the words soulful spaces in a secular, metaphorical way. In speaking of spirituality, John P. Miller (2002) writes, "The Dalai Lama makes a useful distinction here between religion and what he calls secular spirituality. Secular spirituality is primarily concerned with fostering qualities such as wisdom and compassion in human beings" (p. v). Similarly, I see my use of soulfulness in a secular way, in that one does not have to be religious to be soulful, and I believe that soulfulness fosters wisdom and compassion in people.

In the foreword to J. P. Miller's (2000) book, Thomas Moore writes,

> An educated person is someone whose innate being has been led out, enticed and appreciated. Education is not at all the same as teaching. It is accomplished by love and faith in the very soul of the child who stands before us crammed with unmanifested talent. (p. vii)

This is why I began the chapter highlighting the importance of soulful spaces as places and spaces where young people can unfold and create themselves. It is not about an external body imposing their ideas of what is important, but it is about allowing people the holistic space to unfold and create themselves in ways they feel compelled to. Moore goes on to write, "The soul of some children will be revealed in mathematics, some in art, some in politics" (p. vii). The point of course is that we must allow for spaces where children's greatness and genius will thrive, whatever their talents or interests may be.

In asking us to consider this, Moore suggests that we ask ourselves some very fundamental questions. He writes,

> When we educate for the soul, we must reflect on our own values and expectation and then ask ourselves: Are we making little replicas of ourselves, or are we leading forth what was planted in eternity? Are we cramming what we judge

appropriate into the child, or are we loving this new stuff we glimpse in the fresh being in our charge? (pp. vii-viii)

And most insightfully Moore reminds us that "the soul asks faith not control. It is not anxious about the future but enjoys what is emerging in the present" (p. viii). It is in this sense that I use the words soulful spaces, and it is here that I see the value and necessity in creating soulful spaces. In addition to what has been said, in speaking of the soul and timeless learning Miller (2006) writes, "*Soul/Spirit* is defined here as a vital, mysterious energy that can give meaning and purpose to our lives" (p. 5). Again, this highlights the importance of creating soulful spaces for individuals and society at large.

Methodology

Methodologically, this chapter, like most of the book, is both a narrative and a political piece of writing. Narrative has a fairly established tradition, as does political writing, yet some may feel discomfiture with research that self-reflexively names itself as political. Saltmarsh (2009) writes,

> The political dimension of qualitative inquiry can come as quite a surprise to novice researchers (and to more experienced researchers), and may lurk in the background as an often unspoken source of potential discomfiture. For those whose research training has taken place under prevailing empiricist orthodoxies, the very idea of writing politically may sit uncomfortably alongside that of research understood as an objective or "neutral" science. However, scholars across a range of disciplinary fields have been arguing for several decades that there is nothing theoretically or politically neutral about the various methods of inquiry and modes of representation that are encompassed under the rubric of qualitative research (see Denizen & Lincoln, 2007; Ellis et al., 2008). (p. 139)

Despite the discomfiture that some may feel, I believe that it is useful and necessary to position the piece politically to help the reader to better frame and understand the argument.

With respect to narrative, Gannon (2009) writes, "Much narrative research claims empirical authority. Researchers make truth claims about their data, and analyses are grounded in the sense that narratives are real telling by real people about their own real lived experiences" (p. 74). Again, I also consider this book to be a political piece of writing. In a chapter titled "Writing politically," Saltmarsh (2009) writes,

> It is such a politics of truth that mobilizes central debates affecting all professional practice fields, often played out publicly in what are commonly referred to as the "science wars", "history wars", "reading wars" and "culture wars" that have emerged as ongoing sites of contestation. Whose views of science, whose versions of history, whose conceptualizations of literacy, and how we might collectively engage in the interpretation and meaning-making from which images and texts—these issues are central to the "truth games" (Foucault, 2002) at play in these ongoing struggles over epistemological and discursive legitimacy. (p. 141)

For me writing politically in this paper means, in part, engaging the reader in a dialogue about, on the one hand, trusting and respecting young people's right to learn what they want, when they want, how they want, and, on the other hand, imposing an externally directed curriculum on them. I am arguing in favour of the former while at the same time not ignoring the importance of community.

Why I believe that mainstream schooling is not soulful

In this section I will share some reasons why I believe that mainstream schooling is not soulful. To do so, I will look at testing, curriculum, and grading. I will detail this short list to make clear my argument that mainstream schooling is not soulful and that we need to do better for the sake of our young people and our world in general. We need to seriously rethink our child-rearing practices and move toward creating more learner-centered democratic approaches. Again, I am making a moral and ethical argument here. We need to stop imprisoning young people in institutions and think that we are doing them and the world a service by doing so. In his book *The Underground History of American Education: An Intimate Investigation Into the Prison of Modern Schooling* Gatto (2003) argues, in part, how schools are prison-like and how they are not about freedom and liberation but about control and oppression. He writes, "Schools train individuals to respond as a mass. Boys and girls are drilled in being bored, frightened, envious, emotionally needy, generally incomplete" (p. 42). Like Gatto, I see mainstream schooling in a similar way, and I believe that we can and need to do better, and as we will see there are contemporary examples from which we can learn. I see mainstream schooling as spaces and places where young people's bodies, minds, and spirits are being controlled, and in my view, if we truly value participatory democratic practices, then this is not acceptable.

Testing

Unfortunately, the curriculum in mainstream schooling is predetermined and externally imposed. With the increasing commonality of standard exams that all children have to write in the name of accountability, the impact on soulfulness is becoming increasingly negative. The reasons why we are moving to standard examinations are complex, but just to name two: first, as Marshall McLuhan (1964) says, the medium is the message, and second, because it generates huge amounts of money for a powerful few.

With respect to the first point, In *Understanding Media: The Extensions of Man* McLuhan says,

In a culture like ours, long accustomed to splitting and dividing all things as a means of control, it is sometimes a bit of a shock to be reminded that, in operational and practical fact, the medium is the message. This is merely to say that the personal and social consequences of any medium—that is, of any extension of ourselves—result from the new scale that is introduced into our affairs by each extension of ourselves, or by any new technology. (p. 7)

One way of looking at this is that we can use standardized tests because we now have technology that makes this possible and that this technology changes and shapes us. Without the power and tracking capabilities that computers make possible, managing and the logistics of standard tests would simply not be possible.

In terms of cost, the money generated from standardized testing is huge. In a recent interview, Bob Schaeffer, one of the leaders of FairTest, an organization that promotes fair and educationally sensible assessments of students, teachers, and schools, says,

> What we do know is that the three major companies involved in the college and graduate school admissions market, the College Board, Educational Testing Service and ACT, have combined revenues of almost $2 billion per year. Add to that the hundreds of millions of grade K to 12 tests administered in public schools across the nation—due to "No Child Left Behind" every student must take at least 17 before graduating from high school, and many states add additional standardized exam requirements—and the industry size must be in the tens of billions of dollars annually, if not more than $100 billion. These figures only include the direct costs of testing—coaching materials, forms, and scoring. An even greater expense is the immense amount of classroom educator time spent preparing students to take exams, administering them and analyzing their scores. Clearly a tremendous amount of money is being spent on standardized exams which would better be devoted to improving teaching and learning. (Stevens, 2009, para. 11)

Of course, I would go even further than Schaeffer in saying that not only are standardized tests a problem, but so are locally developed and classroom-based tests. They are all hurting learners, young and old alike. The problem with externally imposed tests is that they, and not learners and their individual interests, drive learning. As we have seen, and will continue to see, with learner-centered democratic approaches, it does not have to be this way—there are positive alternatives that are currently being practiced and that mainstream schooling can look to.

Curriculum

For me, the issues around curriculum are among the biggest challenges that need to be addressed if we are serious about creating soulful spaces. One problem with the traditional, schooled curriculum is that it is externally imposed: Others decide what is best for an individual to learn. This is very limiting and harmful. People should be able to choose what they want to learn, when, how, and if they want to learn it. We have a very unfortunate and limited view of what children are like and of what constitutes valuable learning. Mainstream schooling holds that school authorities know what is best for children to learn and that, largely for the sake of the economy and global competitiveness, we need to force children to learn. These assumptions and starting points are problematic on many levels. On an individual level we should allow children to follow their passions and learn what strikes their curiosity and interests—whatever the curriculum they choose may be. On a global level I think we would be better off if we allowed individuals to follow their passions and unfold in their own ways. Imagine if we allowed those with a passion in math to focus on math and those with a passion in literacy to follow that passion and those with a passion in piano to play piano and so on. Clearly, when people have a passion for something they will explore that passion much more thoroughly and with more commitment than those who have no interest in the area. In our world we need diversity and a number of skills, not a standardized, limited, and limiting set. In short, we need a willed curriculum for every child. In addition, still along the lines of global competitiveness, ultimately should it make a difference to us if the cure for cancer or any other debilitating disease comes from our nation state or another? Might not fostering cooperation among children go further in ensuring our individual and collective well-being than constant, senseless competition which ensures that most children fail early and often, typically for no valid intellectual reason, and cease academic pursuits entirely?

As well, I truly believe that an individual will know best what skills they have, what they are capable of, and what they are willing to commit to. Currently, the mainstream system acts as if an external individual or body knows the answer to these questions better than the person who is embodying his or her own holistic space. We need to allow for spaces where people can unfold in ways that they choose, spaces where people are allowed and encouraged to unfold according to their own Being, rather than spaces where individuals are molded to fit the perceived needs of a future that we cannot realistically foresee.

Robinson and Aronica (2009) write, "Children starting school this year will be retiring in 2070. No one has any idea of what the world will look like in ten years' time, let alone in 2070" (p. 17). This is yet another reason why a predetermined, externally imposed curriculum fails; basing a curriculum on the skills and knowledge important in a previous century can hardly serve us well into the future.

Grades

I want to persist and share a few more examples of how mainstream schooling leads to unsoulful spaces just in case my argument is still unclear. In short, grades work against soulful spaces, whether we use the word grade to refer to the segregation of students into cells/classrooms or we use the term to refer to marks. I will speak briefly about both: As I mentioned previously, I have two daughters, born in 2003 and 2005. The one born in 2003 has decided to go to school, and she is happy with her decision thus far and of course she is not stuck with that decision forever. She can choose not to go to school anytime. The child born in 2005 has decided she does not want to go to school, and she is happy with her decision. I see myself as primarily a child advocate, and so I believe that children can be trusted to make substantive decisions about their lives and that they should be supported when they do. I am not a fan of the mainstream school that one of my daughters has decided to attend, but I do support her decision, despite the fact that I disagree with it. The reason why I share this is because my schooled daughter's experience reveals a lot about how placing students in different grades and classes works against soulful spaces. One of her best friends in the whole world, and one of the reasons why she enjoys school, was purposefully separated from her because they are too close. Separating children and not allowing them to interact with children whom they love is not a way of developing soulful spaces.

In fact, we should encourage students to connect with people of all ages and not just their age peers. My children spend time with people of all ages and are richer because of their experiences. Along the same line, my schooled daughter, who is now in grade 2, shared with me how her school principal suggested to her and her grade 2 peers that they should play only among themselves and not with people of different age groups within their school. How is that for building soulfulness?

Here is another example of how souls are torn apart rather than fulfilled in schools. When she was in kindergarten, my daughter mentioned to me how she wished that during the school day she could go in and play with another of her friends who was in a different class and grade. She felt sad and strange that she could not because she did not yet understand, or had not yet assimilated fully into the way schools work; she did not fully understand they were separated into different cells by design. As well, we have friends who are twins, and the school policy is that the twins cannot be in the same class—again these young people are soulmates and, if they had a choice, would want to be together; unfortunately, this is not allowed at the school. When architecture and structures are set up to separate you from interacting with people with whom you want to be, then your soul pays a price. The same goes for being forced to interact only with those who are the same age as you are and to be limited from interacting for so much of the day with those who are much older and much younger than you are.

Giving grades or evaluative marks is just as damaging if we are interested in creating soulful spaces. Grades or marks are harmful in so many ways. For example, they create competition among students and fear within students. Holt (1964/1982) writes,

> We destroy the disinterested (I do not mean uninterested) love of learning in children, which is so strong when they are small, by encouraging and compelling them to work for petty and contemptible rewards—gold stars, or papers marked 100 and tacked to the wall, or A's on report cards, or honor rolls, or dean's lists, or Phi Beta Kappa keys—in short, for the ignoble satisfaction of feeling that they are better than someone else. We encourage them to feel that the end and aim of all they do in school is nothing more than to get a good mark on a test, or to impress someone with what they seem to know. We kill, not only their curiosity, but their feeling that it is a good and admirable thing to be curious, so that by the age of ten most of them will not ask questions, and will show a good deal of scorn for the few who do. (pp. 274–275)

And Llewellyn (1991/1998) writes,

> Bad grades start a vicious circle. They make you feel like a failure. A sense of failure cripples you and prevents you from succeeding. Therefore, you continue to get bad grades and continue to be stifled. (p. 48)

And later she writes, "Good grades are often equally as dangerous. They encourage you to forsake everything worthwhile that you might love, just to keep getting them" (p. 49). Clearly, an environment that results in such trauma cannot be characterized as a soulful space.

I can go on and talk about mainstreaming schooling and assignments, competition, rules, and so on, but I think to do so would not be necessary. Taken individually these obstacles are in themselves problematic—when we look at the picture that I created holistically I believe that the lack of soulfulness in mainstream schooling becomes that much greater. When I use the term mainstream schooling I see it as being more than about a physical space or institution but more of a philosophical discourse that pervades, infects, and informs a worldview. So whether someone is in a bricks and mortar school, a virtual school, or is being home schooled, if they subscribe to a mainstream schooling worldview, then they are subject to the same lack of a soulful space. To clarify, a mainstream schooling worldview is one that is not learner-centered and not democratic. In other words, if young people are in environments where they are prevented from unfolding and creating themselves we must transform these spaces by making them more soulful.

Alternatives

The question then becomes, what are our alternatives? Is there a way that young people can be raised without the trauma inflicted and exacerbated by mainstream schooling and its underlying philosophy? Because the truth is that, whether this way of child rearing happens in schools or in homes or in other contexts, it is just as harmful. In short, the question is, can we create soulful spaces?

Fortunately, the answer is affirmative: Of course we can. Not only can we create these spaces, but they are already there waiting for more of us to embrace them. I believe that learner-centered democratic approaches to child rearing result in spaces that approach soulfulness. I use the term approach because I see the creation of soulful spaces as complex and ongoing and not static and complete. Soulful spaces need to be constantly nurtured.

To clarify, I am using the terms learner-centered and democratic in a way that Jerry Mintz (2004) does. He defines learner-centered education as "an approach that is based on the interest of the student rather than curriculum driven, where someone else has the idea of what you ought to be learning," and he defines democratic education as "education where students are actually empowered to make decisions about their own education and if they are in a school their own school." So, in sum, I believe that learner-centered democratic spaces are soulful spaces.

Free Schools

Sudbury Valley is an example of a learner-centered democratic school. The school was founded in 1968 and is located in Framingham, Massachusetts. With over 200 students, "it is a school where students from preschool through high school age explore the world freely, at their own pace and in their own unique ways" (Individuality and Democracy, n.d.). In March 2009 I was fortunate to be able to visit the school. I have been in countless public and private schools, and it was clear to me from my visit at the Sudbury Valley School that by children being trusted and respected enough to create their own curriculum, more learning and more meaningful learning was happening there than at any other school I have ever been to.

The dynamic and energy of the school was infectious. It was heartwarming to see people of all ages intermingling, interacting, and learning from each other. The school is clearly a soulful place because it has successfully eliminated so many of the limitations of mainstream schooling and is stronger and richer for it. It is amazing to see how younger people learn from older people, and the older from the younger in a way that is natural and seamless. People are free to direct their own learning and therefore can unfold and create themselves in beautiful ways.

When I say "beautiful ways" I do not mean to imply that free schools are issue free but that even the way they resolve their issues is democratic. I have been to several free schools and was fortunate enough to have, on several occasions, been invited to attend their School Meetings and Judicial Committee sessions. In describing the School Meeting, Greenberg (1992) writes,

> The day-to-day life of the school is governed by the School Meeting, both directly and through its various agents. School Meeting consists of all the people at school on a day-to-day basis—namely, all students and staff, each of whom has a vote. (p. 142)

He also describes the Judicial Committee as a space where "the school's disciplinary problems are taken care of in the context of the Judicial System established at the School Meeting . . . . the details of the system are, again, spelled out in the Law Book" (p. 144). For privacy reasons, I do not feel that I can share the content of what I have witnessed in the School Meetings and the Judicial Committees I have sat in on, but suffice it to say that issues do arise and the process is laudable and democratic.

In free schools, young people are not all forced to follow a standard curriculum, they are not graded, and they are not formally tested; yet they are clearly thriving and learning. With respect to reading, for example, which is a current research interest of mine, Gatto (2009) writes,

> To learn to read and to like it takes about thirty contact hours under the right circumstances, sometimes a few more, sometimes a few less. It's a fairly easy skill for anyone to pick up if good reasons to do so are provided. Exhortation isn't sufficient, however, nor intimidation, humiliation, or the confusion of a classroom full of strangers. The only way you can stop a child from learning to read and liking it—in the densely verbal culture which surrounds us all with printed language anywhere we turn—is to teach it the way we teach it [in mainstream schooling]. (p. 152)

In contrast, at Sudbury Valley young people learn to read without being explicitly taught. Elsewhere Gatto (2003) writes,

> In thirty years of operation, Sudbury Valley has never had a single kid who didn't learn to read . . . So Sudbury doesn't even teach reading, yet all its kids learn to read and even like reading. What could be going on there that we don't understand? (p. 58)

When I was at Sudbury Valley, some people were learning alone, others in groups; some were on computers; others were playing sports; others reading books; others talking; others were in a formal class that they decided to attend; others were playing musical instruments; others were just being; and others were playing. Some were inside, others were outside; some were in one room, others in another; some were in one building and others in another. The diversity, complexity, and dynamics of what was happening results in a rich and varied environment. I believe that by having the young people be responsible for their lives and learning, they learn to be responsible. If we are interested in raising responsible adults, they will naturally benefit from freedom and the practice of responsibility when they are young.

One misconception that I often come up against when I share my experiences with being in free schools is that people say to me that having people in an environment without rules will result in chaos. This also comes up with unschooling all the time. People mistakenly think that unschooling parents never say no their kids and that they let the kids do whatever they want. Perhaps comparing and contrasting how this issue plays out in a free school or a Sudbury versus an unschooling environment would be useful. Having no rules may pose a problem, but free schools and Sudbury Valley schools are not places without rules. In fact many free schools probably have more rules than mainstream schools, but the difference and the empowerment come in that the rules are not imposed in an autocratic way but are developed and can be challenged through a democratic process. This works so well at Sudbury Valley that there is no need to have the students under constant surveillance and supervision for fear that in the absence of an adult with authority the young people would be destructive. When at the Sudbury school, I witnessed how the young people were free to move from place to place when they wanted and without the need for constant adult supervision. Again, when issues arise there are democratic and respectful processes in place to deal with the issues: school meetings and judicial committees, for example.

Many of the fears, myths, and the assumptions that mainstream schools operate from are simply not needed in free schools, Sudbury schools, and even in democratic schools. Mainstream schooling's philosophy assumes that children are lazy, destructive, and mean, so a system was created where children are not supported but controlled. For example, that young people are seen as being lazy is why I believe that children are forced and manipulated through grades and bribed with stickers to complete a curriculum that so many find unimportant and irrelevant. Clearly, a system where young people's minds, bodies, and spirits are constantly monitored, surveyed, judged, and corrected is, in short, a place devoid of soul. It does not have to be this way, and soulful places like free schools can be great places and spaces for mainstream schoolers to begin to challenge their own practices; unfortunately, and one of the challenges I face constantly, is that so many people are not even aware that these wonderful spaces exist. Even with many, many academics in faculties of education that I speak to, I find that I have to constantly explain and define what I am referring to and assure people that these places actually exist and are flourishing. Perhaps even more dangerous are those who believe they know all about free schools and have negative views of them, without ever visiting a free school or immersing themselves within the tradition. So having never been to one and knowing little, if anything, about them, they feel that they know one thing, and that is that they do not work. In my mind this naïveté is dangerous because it results in a narrow vision and limited possibilities similar to what we currently have in mainstream schooling, and people will continue to be wounded by it deeply.

These spaces and places are extremely important to include within our world because they are living examples of how different things can be. Change from within is very difficult, but if more and more people demand change and enter these spaces and places that are more learner-centered democratic, then the mainstream schools have to respond to the threat of losing students by offering what the public demands. Unfortunately, we are far from this point now, but I believe the way to change is through external pressures, from parents, children, and learners of all ages, for example. If change is to happen it will happen in a grass roots way, from the bottom up, rather than top down.

What we need is awareness and, more important, more action, more people setting up these spaces. Unfortunately, given the direction and rules and regulations dictated from those with power to control public schooling systems, those who want to create public and therefore financially accessible learner-centered democratic schools are hard pressed. There are several that I am aware of in my neighborhood that are currently trying to create learner-centered democratic schools within the public system, yet are finding it difficult if not impossible, given the rules around grading, curriculum, standardized testing, and so on that are such an ingrained part of mainstream schooling. These rules work directly against free schools and soulful spaces. Despite these challenges, we need to persist, and fortunately there are people doing so even within the mainstream.

Perhaps the most famous example of people in positions of power flexing their authority is connected to Summerhill. In the case of Summerhill, the people in positions of power that I am referring to is the Office for Standards in Education, Children's Services and Skills (OFSTED) which is the nonministerial government department of Her Majesty's Chief Inspector of Schools In England. Summerhill is one of the most famous and successful free schools in the world, and was almost forced to close because there were those in positions of power who, when they inspected the school, found it to deviate too much from their comfortable and familiar worldview.

Fortunately, in the end, and after an expensive court battle, Summerhill was allowed to continue. The frightening thing in all of this is that even if students, parents, teachers, administrators, and the community are supportive of the school, they can easily be overruled. It is unconscionable that the main stakeholders are powerless to raise their children or themselves in ways that they choose. In *Summerhill School: A New View of Childhood* Neill (1992) says,

> Summerhill today (1971) is in essentials what it was when I founded it in 1921. Self-government for the pupils and staff, freedom to go to lessons or stay away, freedom to play for days or weeks or years if necessary, freedom from any indoctrination whether religious or moral or political, freedom from character moulding. (p. 3)

Summerhill is an early, landmark example of a learner-centered democratic space that allows children to unfold and create themselves.

Unschooling or natural learning

As we discussed earlier, another laudable option and one that I am very partial to is unschooling or natural learning. Creating an environment where natural learning is honored is moving in the direction of creating a soulful space. It is not enough to talk about democracy and soulful places and spaces; these discourses need to be practiced, acted on, and embodied. People need to live democratically and soulfully. I truly believe that natural learning does just this. As we discussed earlier, natural learning is usually connected with a way of homeschooling. Natural learners can unfold and follow their own passions and interests rather than an externally imposed and monitored agenda.

Natural learning is about trust and about understanding that humans are natural learners. It is about understanding that there is no critical period for learning and that people will learn best when and about what they choose to learn. Natural learning opens up possibilities rather than being limited to a standardized, one-size–fits-all system. Natural learning recognizes that learning can take place outside institutions and that perhaps the best type of learning is one that happens within genuine contexts. Natural learning is about understanding that the content and the method of learning are not predefined. Natural learning does not place any limits on what and how individuals learn and as a philosophy it allows individuals to unfold and create themselves as they see fit.

I am living and researching natural learning. From this experience I have come to appreciate and respect this peaceful and mindful approach. As I said before, I believe that we all practice natural learning on a daily basis. It is what we do, unconsciously and all the time. What I think needs to happen is that more of us need to recognize it when we do it and to understand it. We need to be mindful and embrace and extend its scope within our lives.

Just to give you a brief example: As mentioned earlier, one area that I am currently interested in is how young people learn to read naturally. The premise is that we should not panic and hurry young people to read but trust and understand that there is no critical period for learning to read and that when young people are ready and motivated they will learn to read gently at their own pace and in their own way.

We need to trust and believe that children can learn to read at their own pace. Priesnitz (2000/2004) highlights this point when she writes:

> The reality is that given a stimulating, trusting environment, and some assistance when requested, children will usually learn to read. One place where these factors come together is England's Summerhill School. Zoe Readhead . . . tells a story about one of the school's instructors. This woman was once a student at the school and did not learn to read until she was a teenager—simply because she did not see the need. Readhead says the woman is grateful that her desire not to learn to read was respected, and that she is now an avid and skilled reader. (p. 79)

In the following quote, Holt (1989) highlights the importance of creating soulful spaces for young people when they are beginning to learn to read,

> In any case, whether you are a "gifted" five-year-old or a terrified, illiterate twelve-year-old, trying to read something new is a dangerous adventure. You may make mistakes, or fail, and so feel disappointment or shame, or anger, or disgust. Just in order to get started on this adventure, most people need as much comfort, reassurance, and security as they can find. The typical classroom, with other children ready to point out, correct, and even laugh at every mistake, and the teacher all too often (wittingly or unwittingly) helping and urging them to do this, is the worst possible place for a child to begin. (p. 3)

As Holt rightly points out, comfort, reassurance, and security are key. But so are interest, freedom, choice, desire, and many other intangible yet important attributes. I truly believe that we need soulful spaces and not competitive environments that do not nurture the soul.

In 2007 I read an article in *Educational Leadership,* an influential educational magazine. I was pleased to find, in a more mainstream publication, support for an approach that is more in line with natural learning than it is with mainstream schooling. In the article, Krashen and McQuillan (2007) write,

> Free voluntary reading means reading because you want to: no book reports, no comprehension questions, and the freedom to put the book down when it is not right for you. It is the kind of reading nearly all literate adults do all the time. (p. 68)

They go on to write that

> correlation studies confirm that students who do more free reading read better, write better, have better grammatical competence, and have larger vocabularies (Krashen, 1997, 2004; McQuillan, 1998) . . . . Much research and many individual cases support the view that late intervention based on free reading can work for struggling readers, that there is no "critical period" for learning to read, and that improvement in literacy can occur at any age. (p. 68)

I won't go into more detail here about the study I am currently conducting because the study is still in progress, but I have been collecting data from people on list serves and analyzing their posted statements about how their children learned to read naturally and at their own pace. My preliminary analysis suggests that those who practice natural learning learn to read without being hurried, at their own pace, and in ways that are very different from how schoolers do. The focus is more on following the learner's lead rather than having the learner follow a prescribed, standardized program. Similarly, in a book titled *How Children Learn at Home,* Thomas and Pattison (2007) explore how children successfully learn at home naturally and in ways that are different from the mainstream schooling ways of teaching and learning. As well, if we make a distinction between literacy and reading where reading is reading for enjoyment and literacy is reading on someone else's terms, and where often understanding is reduced to what is measurable, it seems that natural learners actively enjoy reading. For example, at my local neighborhood school the students scored above the provincial average on a standardized test that measures literacy, but the students scored below the provincial average on a self-reported survey that they fill out before writing the test and reported that they disliked reading. This leads me to question whether it is enough to create a literate population if they do not like to read and choose not to read. In other words, is it an accomplishment that they score high on a literacy test while at the same time reporting that they do not like to read and, in fact, don't read? More specifically, when asked if they like to read, 47% of students at this school responded yes, in comparison to 65% within the board and 59% provincially. This is the result in a school where 77% of students scored at or above the provincial standard on a province wide reading test, in a school board where 57% did, and a province where 61% did; so, in comparison the students scored well on the literacy portion of the test, but what is the point if in the end they dislike reading? In contrast, those who learn to read naturally tend to self-report that they enjoy reading. I understand the limitations to this simplistic analysis, but I am just as interested in raising questions as in presenting definitive conclusions. More analysis and research are required, but I believe the questions are worth investigating.

In the case of my own daughter, the one born in 2005, she is teaching me about the power of letting children teach themselves. Watching her learn on her own seems magical because of my conditioning, but really it is natural and no big deal. For example, the words she knows are not the ones chosen by an external authority and placed on a word wall but are an active part of her world. She can spell "I love you," because she leaves me notes with that message everywhere; she can spell "stop" because she notices stop signs in her world, and "open" because she sees "open" signs on store fronts, and the same applies to the hundreds of other words I know she knows and the many more that I am not even aware of. The other day my older daughter was writing a silly story about me and wanted to know how to spell "poop," and the younger piped in "p-o-o-p." She knows how to spell poop because her favorite book is titled *Everyone Poops* by Taro Gomi (1977/1993). She likes it so much that she made a copy of it by hand for my wife's upcoming birthday. It was all her idea, and she drew the pictures and copied the words and asked for limited help when she felt she needed it. It took her months, and she worked on it whenever she felt like it, but she did it. She was 4 at the time.

In a recent newspaper article by Hammer (2011), she writes, "The reason the American approach doesn't work? If children are pushed to read, for example, they might learn at an earlier age but research suggests they're also more likely to become disinterested in reading by the age of eight" (p. A12). She then goes on to quote Professor Marilyn Chapman, an early learning expert at the University of British Columbia, as saying, "At the end of the day they don't like reading and writing and then they don't want to do it unless they're forced to; what's the point?" Indeed, what's the point?

Conclusion

Epstein (2007) writes,

One would think that military personnel—obligated to follow orders without question—and prisoners—stripped of most of their rights by the criminal justice system—would be far more encumbered than noninstitutionalized teens. But that's not what I found . . . In other words, *teens appear to be subjected to about twice as many restrictions as are prisoners and soldiers and to more than ten times as many restrictions as are everyday adults.* (p. 11)

Although Epstein's study focused on teens, the same disrespect applies to those even younger. To have young people live with so many restrictions, more than even prisoners, is, to me, a clear indication that the spaces they are currently living in cannot be characterized as being soulful spaces. We have the technology, the know-how, and the models already in existence; now all more of us need is to have the courage and the will to choose and demand soulful spaces rather than those that lack soulfulness.

11 CONCLUSION

I believe that mutual love, mutual trust, mutual respect, and mutual compassion will result in people who are more loving, trusting, respectful, and compassionate toward themselves, other people, beings, and things in the world.

In the past few months, about 50 media representatives from various radio, newspapers, television, and on-line organizations have contacted me. The reason I mention this is that since I was first interested in learner-centered democratic approaches to learning, I have noticed the interest and reaction to the wonders of this philosophy growing dramatically and becoming more positive, to my delight.

As a child advocate, I believe that our current state of child-rearing and schooling is shameful—we should and can do much better. Unfortunately, far too often I still notice young people being force-fed, yelled at, disciplined, and controlled even when they are clearly in the right. They are being forced to dress in certain ways, forced to attend programs and activities that they would rather not attend, and so on. Young people's minds, bodies, emotions, and spirits are controlled in ways that can only be described as shameful. Young people are among the last "acceptably" oppressed group—we can do things to children that we would never dream of doing to another adult human being. One way to correct this oppression is to take seriously learner-centered democratic approaches to learning, education, and life. We need to take the power and ethic of the willed curriculum seriously.

Learner-centered approaches to learning are based on the assumption that learners themselves get to decide what, when, where, and how they want to learn as well as deciding when they want to opt in and when they want to opt out. While this may sound like an extraordinary amount of freedom in a typical American, Canadian, or world context, in practice, learner-centered democratic education means that children are deeply engaged in what they learn, self-motivated beyond what we typically see in most students, and able to sort through learning problems because they have a great deal of confidence in themselves as learners. Unschooling sees life as the curriculum. Some argue that the world is a school, but the world is not a school. It is our birthright, our environment, our habitat, and we live and learn seamlessly in it. It is school that divides living from learning. With the willed curriculum nothing is ruled out, and nothing is imposed. The learner decides what is needed. It could be a workbook, a formal school, or a skate park. The democratic part is that they have a substantive say in running the places and spaces that they inhabit as learners. In part, learner-centered democratic schooling as a pedagogical approach arises out of some of the radical school movements of the 1960s and 1970s and now is a fully flowered "movement" with many types of schools, practitioners, and "graduates."

So unschooling, also known as organic learning, natural learning, open source learning, and life learning, is particularly promising because it allows learners to be self-directed, self-organizing, and to take control of their learning and their lives. As well, it allows young people to follow their internal motivation, which in turn translates into doing what one loves, and allows learners to unfold and create themselves in ways that they choose.

The willed curriculum is a philosophy, a worldview, a way of life. It can take place outside of formal schooling or within. It allows the learner to decide what type of curriculum he/she would like to subscribe to. For example, my two children have benefited by living a willed philosophy. I have learned a great deal from them and from others who follow a similar approach. My older daughter has decided that she wants to attend mainstream schooling, and so she does, and my younger has decided that she wants to learn outside of schooling, and so she does. To date they are both happy with their decisions, and as a child advocate who takes young people's voices seriously I support their decisions. When my younger daughter was 4, we purchased a formal curriculum workbook and offered it to her. It basically covered the curriculum for 5- to 6-year-olds. The idea that schools are the only place to get the traditional mainstream schooling curriculum is no longer true. In fact these books are hundreds of pages in length and cover the curriculum in every subject and for every grade. The costs for these workbooks are between $10 and $20 per curriculum year. So, even if you buy into the myth of the schooling curriculum, there are easy ways of getting it. In fact, at my daughter's school her classroom teacher makes use of these workbooks. Since we have copies, we know that what she sometimes sends home is right out of these books. As mentioned earlier, because she wanted to, my younger daughter completed the whole curriculum in a few mornings and moved on. The books are fairly comprehensive and cover all of the traditional school subjects. They are based and created on Ministry of Education guidelines.

Remarkably, given our biases about the need to have an externally imposed curriculum, my daughters create a much more rigorous and organic curriculum for themselves than I, who have a PhD in curriculum, or anyone else can ever create for them. My children play—they play a lot with friends inside and outside, at our house and at their friends' places, they dance, sing, play music, get dressed, shower, make their own snacks, write, read, watch television, use the computer, and, in short, do what John Holt defines as learning: they live life, and as they live their lives they learn things.

Perhaps the greatest and saddest criticism of unschooling is that not all people come from good homes, and so what do we do with people who do not have the same advantages as others? This is a legitimate concern, and as a society we need to do, and can do, much better at helping those who are suffering or who have been traditionally marginalized. The problem with this argument is that people normally see the solution as a dual one. Since their home life is unsafe, then we need to send them to mainstream schools. This argument is limiting and flawed. In fact, this demographic is the one that is served least well by mainstream schooling, and so sending young people from one obstacle into another is not the solution. The solution is not an *either or*, but a *what else can be done*? Some argue that children who have abusive parents find mainstream schools a place of love and support, and they feel safe there. Unfortunately, it is these students that struggle in school, and so the argument quickly falls apart. We can and need to do much better with all students in mainstream schools and should work especially hard to ensure that students who have out-of-school challenges are treated with love, trust, respect, care, and compassion.

The willed curriculum is about love, trust, respect, care, and compassion. It is about allowing young people to unfold and create themselves in ways that are driven by their souls, their spirits, and their internal motivation. It is about allowing young people, and all people, to learn in the world, to use whatever available resources, methods, and tools the learner chooses.

I think we need to do what Kohn (2010) recently suggested in an article. He suggests that we need to focus on "students' achievements (the intellectual accomplishments of individual kids)," rather than only on "student achievement (the aggregate results of standardized tests)" (para. 8). The goal, one that is also pointed out by Holt, is that we need to make unschooling and other learner-centered democratic environments, like free schools and Sudbury schools, and democratic schools, a legitimate and accessible option for learners.

As an unschooling parent, when issues and disagreements arise we trust that a democratic process will help us resolve our differences. For example, consider the following: Should a five-year-old go to bed whenever s/he likes? My response is yes; however, the understanding needs to be that there are other people's wants and needs that have to be considered. For instance, the child may want to stay up, but others may want to go to sleep. In addition, if the child does not get enough sleep, and is grumpy the next day, and it impacts others, then this also needs to be considered. Ultimately, the adult should not therefore impose a bedtime, but these things should be discussed and worked out in a mutually agreeable way. One solution might be that the child can stay up while others go to sleep but must be quiet enough not to awaken others.

In short, we try to hear all sides, and it is not unusual that after democratically airing issues, the younger people in my family convince the older that they were right and that the older people were wrong. This does not diminish the adults' wisdom but increases it by understanding that all humans are wise and that sometimes we have to listen and be prepared to change our minds. This is not a sign of weakness but of strength.

Understanding the power of the willed curriculum has changed my life by giving me the strength and the confidence to continue to do what I do and to advocate for young people. It has taught me that young people can and should be trusted just as much as adults to make appropriate decisions; that learning and schooling are not the same things; that learning can and does happen anytime, anyplace, and from anyone; that learning can happen without tests, grades, assignments, marks, classrooms, bells, and so on.

I believe that those who are truly interested in making soulful connections with other human beings will do well to learn more about the willed curriculum and other learner-centered democratic approaches. For those who want to learn more, I recommend reading anything by John Holt, but particularly *Learning all the Time* (1989). Teachers, principals, superintendents, and leaders in public schooling need embodied proof that children can learn in different ways, in more respectful, loving, compassionate, and trusting ways which will result in more humane and soulful connections and positive growth to our minds, bodies, emotions, and spirits. By questioning so much of what mainstream schooling sees as self-evident, the willed curriculum, I believe, can help mainstream schools make positive changes by inspiring a move towards learner-centered democratic ways.

As we saw, some critics are concerned that a willed approach such as unschooling can make children too self-focused. Some caution that unschoolers may become too concerned about the individual while ignoring the community. I believe that this is not the case in practice. Unschoolers learn to be responsible, compassionate, and democratic, not by reading about or being told about this but by actually living it. The unschoolers that I have met support this. They are confident, social, and very respectful. This comes from living the unschooling life. A large part of unschooling is about respecting others, responsibility, freedom, and democratic living. After meeting many unschooled students, it becomes clear that community and community service are of huge importance.

I believe that a one-size-fits-all model that tries to convince us that a single, externally imposed curriculum that everyone has to ingest is seriously misguided; this model ought to be replaced with a model that trusts learners and respects everyone's needs and interests. We have to stop taking drumsticks away from the Justin Biebers of the world and hockey sticks away from the Sidney Crosbys, and we must stop trying to convince them that they should instead be embracing pens and pencils. A schooling that is consistent with the classic ads that claim that it tastes bad but it works is not a good model for learners. Learning, unlike some types of medicine, does not have to taste bad to work. If trusted and respected, people will naturally gravitate to where their interests and passions lie. The result will be a much more focused and rigorous curriculum for everyone. Again, this is not only possible but it is happening, and we need to embrace the models that are in place and not set obstacles in their way and make things more difficult for them.

As well, we should not confuse grades with competence. Simply because you have the highest grade does not mean that you are the most competent, and simply because you pass a paper and pencil test about haircutting does not mean you can practice haircutting, for example.

People are often told that they are where they are because of their schooling. I for one am not where I am because of schooling. I am where I am because of me, and what I learned, and the people and ways I learned from outside of schooling. As I mentioned earlier, schooling was an obstacle, not a help. Even if you believe that schooling is the answer, then you can get to where you want to be with a lot less schooling. If schools were responsible for where I am today, then what of the many other people who were schooled alongside me and have ended up in different career paths? Some are happy with where they are, and others less so. So, clearly it's not the schooling; it's infinitely more complicated. And as Arum and Rosaka (2011) point out in their book *Academically Adrift: Limited Learning on College Campuses*, higher education does not turn most students into better reasoners and thinkers.

Another argument some critics raise has to do with fairness. For example, if one student does nothing or little and another student does a lot, is it fair that they receive the same grade? First, the assumption is that the purpose of schooling is to grade and rank and not to learn. If the learning is most important, then the person who learns and gets the most out of it is better off because of that and not because of the grade. You can learn more and yet be graded lower. In addition, suppose someone had more of an interest, should the person with less of an interest be punished for having less of an interest if the curriculum does not resonate with her/him?

As well, imagine as a chiropractor that you really want to learn more about working on the knee, either because that is your strength or because it is your weakness, and you take a course and the course is about shoulders, something you have little need for or interest in. Would you not be better off if you were allowed to work on learning more about knees and let someone else in the course, who has an interest and or need to work on shoulders, to learn about working on shoulders? The same applies to all other forms of learning; if someone feels that they need to work on learning math, then that is where they should focus their efforts, regardless of the title of the course or what the curriculum mandates.

To conclude, I want to say more about unschooling, since I believe it is the best learning model we currently have that offers the greatest possibility for love, trust, respect, care, and compassion. Unschooling is what we decide it is. It is not something neutral but a constructed worldview. The stories we share and tell about unschooling ultimately define what unschooling is. This book, in part, is an attempt to start a serious conversation about what unschooling is, what it can be, and what it ought to be. As unschoolers, we can ultimately define and shape what it becomes. Unschooling is a disruptive innovation in a very positive sense. Unschooling is challenging our current assumptions about learning and living and forcing us to rethink and reinvent how learning and living (and everything that surrounds it) happens.

We now live at a time when we do not have to wait for a program to happen on television, but we can watch it on demand. This notion of on-demand watching is connected to unschooling as an on-demand learning philosophy. The curriculum needs to be individualized and on-demand, and schools need to catch up to this new reality or risk becoming increasingly obsolete and disconnected from the way the world works. If I want to learn about X, it does not make sense for me to have to wait until grade Y to learn about it. Our on-demand world insists that we have access to information whenever we need it. This new and exciting reality is what schools have to incorporate into their realities. This means that an externally imposed curriculum taught to a large group needs to be replaced by an individualized curriculum that is constantly emerging and being tweaked by the learner who wills it. If schools ignore this reality, if they insist on doing things the same way and in the same places, I would like to think that they are speeding the way to their demise.

Not only does the curriculum have to be willed, but the place where it is being presented also needs to be flexible, given our current realities. No longer is it convincing that learning is something that necessitates a learner bringing her/his body to an institution. Learning can and does now happen anyplace, anytime, and by anyone. Whether it is using smart technology or walking down the street, learning happens all around us, and this reality needs to be tapped, not ignored. The willed curriculum recognizes this and encourages learners to learn from anyone or anyplace at anytime. As advocates of the willed curriculum we need to facilitate this and not prevent learning from happening by insisting that all young people between the ages of 6 and 18 need to confine their bodies to a particular place for a set number of hours a day. This does not advance learning, but stifles it. In contrast, the willed curriculum demands that we recognize that learning happens as we live our lives, and the richer and more varied our lived lives are the more learning can happen. Sitting in a room, being forced to learn things we have little interest in and that we do not choose is clearly not a rich experience. The willed curriculum is at the fore of a renewed understanding about learning, teaching, education, and living, which makes it very exciting and innovative. The willed curriculum is a philosophy grounded in respect, holism, compassion, mindfulness, soulfulness, interconnectedness, and, most important of all, love. Ultimately, the purpose of this book is to reignite conversations, to see where we stand, and how we need to move forward, for both unschoolers and schoolers alike. In short, it is for anyone interested in raising children in more democratic and gentle, yet powerful ways. Please join me in moving towards gentler willed approaches and away from harsher ones.

REFERENCES

Arum, R., & Rosaka, J. (2011). *Academically adrift: Limited learning on college campuses.* Chicago, IL: University of Chicago Press.

Bevans, K., Fitzpatrick, L.-A., Sanchez, B., & Forrest, C. B. (2010). Individual and instructional determinants of student engagement in physical education. *Journal of Teaching in Physical Education, 29*, 399–416.

Brown, L. (2011, June 22). The fourth R—Helping stressed-out students relax. *The Toronto Star.* Retrieved from http://www.parentcentral.ca/parent/education/article/1012768--the-fourth-r-helping-stressed-out-students-relax

Chu, J. M. (Director). (2011). *Justin Bieber: Never say never* [DVD].

Craig, W., & Pepler, D. (1998). Observation of bullying and victimization in the school yard. *Canadian Journal of Psychology, 13*(2), 41–59.

Csikszentmihalyi, M. (1997). *Finding flow: The psychology of engagement with everyday life.* New York, NY: BasicBooks.

Davis, M. (2010, September 10). *Mathew Davis on unschooling* [Video file].
Retrieved from http://www.youtube.com/UnschoolingChannel#p/u/2/y8wftcGid0c

Epstein, R. (2007). *The case against adolescence: Rediscovering the adult in every teen.* Sanger, California: Quill Driver Books/Word Dancer Press.

Farenga, P. (2010, September 9). Pat Farenga on unschooling

[Video file]. Retrieved from http://www.youtube.com/UnschoolingChannel#p/u/4/tl-A21hFaF0

Freire, P. (1998). *Pedagogy of freedom: Ethics, democracy, and civic courage.* Lanham, MD: Rowman & Littlefield.

Freire, P. (2000). *Pedagogy of the oppressed.* New York, NY: Continuum International. (Original work published 1970)

Gannon, S. (2009). Writing narrative. In J. Higgs, D. Horsfall, & S. Grace (Eds.), *Writing qualitative research on practice* (pp. 73–82). Rotterdam, The Netherlands: Sense.

Gardner, H. (2011). *Frames of mind: The theory of multiple intelligences.* New York, NY: Basic Books. (10th Anniversary ed.) with new introduction.

Gatto, J. T. (2003). *The underground history of American education: An intimate investigation into the prison of modern schooling* (Rev. ed.). Oxford, New York: Oxford Village Press.

Gatto, J. T. (2005). *Dumbing us down: The hidden curriculum of compulsory schooling.* Gabriola Island, BC: New Society. (Original work published 1992)

Gatto, J. T. (2009). *Weapons of mass instruction: A schoolteachers' journey through the dark world of compulsory schooling.* Gabriola Island, BC: New Society.

Gatto, J. T. (2010a, September 9). *John Taylor Gatto on unschooling—part 1* [Video file]. Retrieved from http://www.youtube.com/UnschoolingChannel#p/u/8/N1xuXomtZr4

Gatto, J. T. (2010b, September 9). *John Taylor Gatto on unschooling—part 2* [Video file]. Retrieved from http://www.youtube.com/UnschoolingChannel#p/u/7/NhbPtJsFxO0

Giroux, H. (2000). *Impure acts: The practical politics of cultural studies.* London, UK: Routledge.

Gomi, T. (1993). *Everyone poops* (A. M. Stinchecum, Trans.). Brooklyn, NY: Miller Book. (Original work published in 1977)

Greenberg, D. (1992). How the school is governed; Who

cares? In *The Sudbury ValleyExperience* (3rd ed., pp. 140–145). Framingham, MA: Sudbury Valley School Press.

Hanh, T. N. (1987). *The Miracle of Mindfulness: A Manual on meditation* (trans: Moby Ho). Boston: Beacon Press. (Original work published 1975)

Hammer, K. (2011, June 14). How play-based learning can lead to more successful kids. *The Globe and Mail*, p. A12.

Holt, J. (1982). *How children fail.* Cambridge, MA: Da Capo Press. (Original work published 1964)

Holt, J. (1983). *How children learn* (Rev. ed.). Cambridge, MA: Da Capo Press. (Original work published 1967)

Holt, J. (1989). *Learning all the time: How small children begin to read, write, count, and investigate the world, without being taught.* Cambridge, MA: Da Capo Press.

Holt, J. (1999). *Growing without schooling: A record of a grassroots movement—Volume one August 1977-December 1979 GWS #1-12.* Cambridge, MA: Holt Associates.

Holt, J., & Farenga, P. (2003). *Teach your own: The John Holt book of homeschooling.* Cambridge, MA.: Da Capo Press.

hooks, b. (2000). *All about love: New visions.* New York, NY: HarperCollins.

Individuality and democracy. (n.d.). *Individuality and democracy: A way of life.* Retrieved from http://www.sudval.org/

International Narcotics Control Board. (2010). *Report of the International Narcotics Control Board on the availability of internationally controlled drugs: Ensuring adequate access for medical and scientific purposes.* Retrieved from http://www.incb.org/pdf/annual-report/2010/en/supp/AR10_Supp_E.pdf

Kincheloe, J. (2004). *Multiple intelligences reconsidered.* New York, NY: Peter Lang.

King, M. L. (2010). *Strength to love.* Minneapolis, MN: Fortress Press. (Original work published 1963)

Kohn, A. (2005). *Unconditional parenting: Moving from rewards and punishments to love and reason.* New York, NY: Atria books.

Kohn, A. (2010, September 17). Schools would be great if it

weren't for the kids. *Washington Post.* Retrieved from http://voices.washingtonpost.com/answer-sheet/guest-bloggers/schools-would-be-great-if-it-w.html#more

Kohn, A. (2011). Challenging students—and how to have more of them. In A. Kohn(Ed.), *Feel-bad education and other contrarian essays on children and schooling.* Boston, MA: Beacon Press.

Krashen, S. (1997). Bridging inequity with books. *Educational Leadership, 55*(4),18–22.

Krashen, S. (2004). False claims about literacy development. *Educational Leadership, 61*(6), 18–21.

Krashen, S., & McQuillan, J. (2007, October). The case for late intervention: Appealing books and no timetable are all some students need to break through reading. Educational Leadership, 65(2), 68-73.

Llewellyn, G. (1991/1998). *The teenage liberation handbook: How to quit school and get a real life and education* (2nd ed.). Eugene, OR: Lowry House.

McLuhan, M. (1964). *Understanding media: The extensions of man.* New York, NY: McGraw Hill.

McQuillan, J. (1998). *The literacy crisis: False claims and real solutions.* Portsmouth, NH: Heinemann.

Miller, J. P. (2000). *Education and the soul: Toward a spiritual curriculum.* Albany: State University of New York Press.

Miller, J. P. (2006). *Educating for wisdom and compassion: Creating conditions for timeless learning.* Thousand Oaks, CA: Corwin Press.

Miller, J. P. (2010). *Whole child education.* Toronto, ON: University of Toronto Press.

Miller, J. P., & Nakagawa, Y. (2002). *Nurturing our wholeness: Perspectives on spirituality in education.* Rutland, VT: The Foundation for Educational Renewal.

Miller, R. (1990). *What are schools for? Holistic education in American culture.* Brandon, VT: Holistic Education Press.

Miller, R. (2002). *Free schools, free people: Education and democracy after the 1960s*. Albany: State University of New York Press.

Miller, R. (2008). *The self-organizing revolution: Common principles of the educational alternatives movement*. Brandon, VT: Psychology Press/Holistic Education Press.

Miller, R. (2010, September 9). *Dr. Ron Miller on unschooling* [Video file]. Retrieved from http://www.youtube.com/UnschoolingChannel#p/u/3/tQUx1LWzPNw

Mintz, J. (1995). *The almanac of education choices: Private and public learning alternatives and homeschooling*. New York, NY: Macmillan.

Mintz, J. (Speaker). (2004, July 28). Building democratic schools. Radio Free School. Retrieved from http://www.radio4all.net/pub/archive/04.01.05/grassroots@hwcn.org/125-1-20040729-0728rfsc10.mp3

Mintz, J. (1994). *Handbook of alternative education*. New York, NY: Macmillan.

Mintz, J. (2010, September 9). *Jerry Mintz on unschooling* [Video file]. Retrieved from http://www.youtube.com/UnschoolingChannel#p/u/6/ZB2y3rx_vUY

Mintz, J. (2003). *No homework and recess all day: How to have freedom and democracy in education*. Roslyn Heights, NY: Bravura Books.

Mintz, J., & Ricci, C. (Eds.). (2010). *Turning points: 35 educational visionaries in education tell their own stories*. USA: AERO.

Neill. A. S. (1992). *Summerhill School: A new view of childhood* (Rev. ed.). New York, NY: St. Martin's Griffin.

Noddings, N. (2003). *Caring: A feminine approach to ethics and moral education* (2nd ed.). Los Angeles: University of California Press. (Original worl published 1984)

Olson, K. (2009). *Wounded by school: Recapturing the joy in learning and standing up to old school culture*. New York, NY: Teachers College Press.

Ontario Ministry of Education. (2010-2011). *Full-day early learning kindergarten program 2010-2011.* Toronto, ON: Ontario Ministry of Education. Retrieved from http://www.edu.gov.on.ca/eng/curriculum/elementary/kindergarten_english_june3.pdf

Philips, C. (2007). *Socrates in love: Philosophy for a die-hard romantic.* New York, NY: W. W. Norton.

Priesnitz, W. (2004). *Challenging assumptions in education.* Toronto, ON: The Alternate Press. (Original work published 2000)

Priesnitz, W. (2011, May/June). Questioning socialization. *Life Learning Magazine,* 18–21.

Ricci. C. (2008). Open universities: You do not need a high school diploma to get into university. *Journal of Unschooling and Alternative Learning.* Retrieved January 25, 2008, from http://www.nipissingu.ca/jual/PDF/v211.pdf., (2)3, (16 pages)

Robinson, K., & Aronica, L. (2009). The element: How finding your passion changes everything. New York, NY: Viking.

Rolstad, K. (2010, September 9). *Dr. Kellie Rolstad on unschooling* [Video file]. Retrieved from http://www.youtube.com/UnschoolingChannel#p/u/5/rln6YvyOnZI

Saltmarsh, S. (2009). Writing politically: Reflections on the writing of politics and the politics of writing. In J. Higgs, D. Horsfall, & S. Grace (Eds.), *Writing qualitative research on practice* (pp. 139–152). Rotterdam, The Netherlands: Sense.

Stevens, T. (2009, June 3). *Re: FairTest—An interview with Bob Schaeffer* [Weblog message. Retrieved from http://abettereducation.blogspot.com/2009/06/fairtest-interview-with-bob-schaeffer.html

Thomas, A., & Pattison, H. (2007). How children learn at home. London, UK: Continuum International Publishing Group.

Tolstoy, L. (1995). *War and peace.* Hertfordshire, Great Britain: Wordsworth Editions.

Weldon. L. G. (2010). *Free range learning: How homeschooling changes everything.* Prescott, AZ: Hohm Press.

Worden, J. M., Hinton, C., & Fischer, K. W. (2011). What does the brain have to do with learning. *Phi Delta Kappan, 92*(8), 8–13.

ABOUT THE AUTHOR

Carlo Ricci earned his PhD in 2003 from the Ontario Institute for Studies in Education of the University of Toronto. Currently he teaches in the Graduate Program at the Schulich School of Education, Nipissing University. He edits and founded the *Journal of Unschooling and Alternative Learning*. He has written and edited a number of books including *Turning Points: 35 Visionaries in Education Tell Their Own Stories* (AERO, 2010) with Jerry Mintz. He has also written numerous articles on unschooling and self-directed learning. He lives in Toronto, Ontario with his wife and two children.

Made in the USA
Lexington, KY
08 March 2014